THE NOTORIOUS B.I.G.

Recent Titles in Greenwood Biographies

THE NOTORIOUS B.I.G.

A Biography

Holly Lang

GREENWOOD BIOGRAPHIES

GREENWOOD PRESS
WESTPORT, CONNECTICUT • LONDON

Library of Congress Cataloging-in-Publication Data

Lang, Holly.
The Notorious B.I.G. : a biography / Holly Lang.
    p. cm. — (Greenwood biographies, ISSN 1540–4900)
  Includes bibliographical references (p.) and index.
  ISBN-13: 978-0-313-34156-4 (alk. paper)
  1. Notorious B.I.G. (Musician)   2. Rap musicians—United States—Biography.
I. Title.
  ML420.N76L36   2007
  782.421649092—dc22   2007029562
  [B]

British Library Cataloguing in Publication Data is available.

Library of Congress Catalog Card Number: 2007029562

ISBN-13: 978-0-313-34156-4
ISSN: 1540–4900

First published in 2007

Greenwood Press, 88 Post Road West, Westport, CT 06881
An imprint of Greenwood Publishing Group, Inc.
www.greenwood.com

Printed in the United States of America

The paper used in this book complies with the
Permanent Paper Standard issued by the National
Information Standards Organization (Z39.48–1984).

10 9 8 7 6 5 4 3 2 1

CONTENTS

Photo essay follows page 62

SERIES FOREWORD

In response to high school and public library needs, Greenwood developed this distinguished series of full-length biographies specifically for student use. Prepared by field experts and professionals, these engaging biographies are tailored for high school students who need challenging yet accessible biographies. Ideal for secondary school assignments, the length, format, and subject areas are designed to meet educators' requirements and students' interests.

Greenwood offers an extensive selection of biographies spanning all curriculum-related subject areas including social studies, the sciences, literature and the arts, and history and politics, as well as popular culture, covering public figures and famous personalities from all time periods and backgrounds, both historic and contemporary, who have made an impact on American or world culture. Greenwood biographies were chosen based on comprehensive feedback from librarians and educators. Consideration was given to both curriculum relevance and inherent interest. The result is an intriguing mix of the well-known and the unexpected, the saints and sinners from long-ago history and contemporary pop culture. Readers will find a wide array of subject choices, from fascinating crime figures such as Al Capone to inspiring pioneers such as Margaret Mead, from the greatest minds of our time, such as Stephen Hawking, to the most amazing success stories of our day, such as that of J. K. Rowling.

Although the emphasis is on fact, not glorification, the books are meant to be fun to read. Each volume provides in-depth information about the subject's life, from birth through childhood, the teen years, and adulthood. A thorough account relates family background and education, traces personal and professional influences, and explores struggles, accomplishments, and contributions. A timeline highlights the most significant life events against a historical perspective. Bibliographies supplement the reference value of each volume.

INTRODUCTION

Easily one of the most revered rappers of all time, Christopher Wallace, better known as the Notorious B.I.G., impacted hip-hop in a way most can only dream. An artist in the true sense, Wallace constructed rhymes that reflected his life, at first focusing strongly on the struggles of the inner-city crack dealer and later reveling in the mafia-style fantasies that would soon become his real life. He was a driving force of this mafioso style of rap, a brand of storytelling that would soon dominate the genre. He also drove hip-hop's popularity in the mainstream markets, producing hits that found their way onto mix tapes just as they found their way into radio rotation. Wallace's influence still is strong more than 10 years after his death, his name a constant in the many hip-hop hot lists.

In his short life, Wallace recorded two albums, both of which are recognized as two of the best-selling releases in rap history. He has had several no. 1 singles on the Billboard Hot 100 and rap charts, and his music has permeated the depths of American culture, his influence spreading across the country as his songs grew in popularity, many of which are still heard on the radio today. His triumphs—both monetary and stylistically—built Bad Boy Records, one of the most successful record labels in history, a company whose influence is widespread not only in hip-hop but in the music industry as a whole. He was a mentor to many rappers, including the now-famous Lil' Kim, and he helped Junior M.A.F.I.A. rise to prominence in the hip-hop world. Even after his death, more albums featuring Wallace were released, almost all instant hits that ranked high on the charts, an unlikely feat for an overweight drug dealer from New York.

From his beginnings on the crack-infested streets of Brooklyn's Bedford-Stuyvesant neighborhood, Wallace always held strong promise, even when his life derailed after he became a petty hustler, slinging crack in New York and North Carolina, or after his two jail stints, one of which spanned nine months. As a way to simply survive, he began to rhyme, weaving into his lyrics the struggles he faced daily—his mother's breast cancer, his ex-girlfriend's accidental pregnancy—events that not only shaped his life but also went on to shape the way rappers approached their art, using autobiographical elements that before were seen only in stripped-down versions of gangsta rap.

Throughout his brief—but prolific—career, Wallace brought rap back to New York, having wrestled back the spotlight from the West Coast, where the gangsta rap created by N.W.A. held the nation's attention. Although graphic in nature, Wallace's lyrics were graceful, as was his delivery, his voice grave as he delivered lines with ease. But as his popularity grew, so did the violence surrounding the genre of rap, triggering a feud that spread across the nation, pitting coast against coast. Eventually, this violence resulted in his death, a murder that is still unsolved, steeped in controversy, and being battled out in California courts. His death also sparked the Rampart scandal, after the circumstances around his murder brought to light the largest known corruption rings in the history of the Los Angeles Police Department. Officers' involvement in crimes ranging from bank robberies to drug dealings to murder were uncovered in the wake of Wallace's death, and more than 70 officers were eventually indicted.

But even despite the controversy, Wallace's story is important to anyone who has ever struggled to survive and dreamed of succeeding because his is the ultimate story of success in the face of incredible odds. His music has shaped American culture the same as it has hip-hop, and his style still bears influence on the industry today. His death, like that of adversary Tupac Shakur, shows the power of thought and of what can happen when someone seeks to live the story he has created, believing in the hype he has manufactured.

As an artist, he brought to rap a narrative approach that soon dominated the New York style, a form that now dominates the rap world. His story as a man is one that reaches almost all aspects of American life, whether through the struggles of his immigrant, single mother, or his life as a petty hustler, or the poor choices he made, or his successes an entire industry felt.

His is the story of an unexpected success born of the sheer necessity to survive and of a life firmly focused on inevitable death, as evidenced by both his album's titles—1994's *Ready to Die* and 1997's *Life after Death*. In the former, his art imitated his life as he recounted the routine details of drug deals, from bagging to selling, and the realization that his growing popularity and success would make him an easy target for hate. The album is filled with references to suicide and eventually ends with his self-imposed death, a melodic, lyrical demise that only Wallace could imagine. Even so, the album carries the promise of hope and the will to keep moving forward, even when it is another day, another struggle.

In *Life after Death*, Wallace took us with him into the world of the gangster, an image largely constructed from popular characters in mafia movies. But that world became eerily familiar as his fame grew, and a bicoastal rap rivalry led to shootouts and showdowns, threats, and eventually, death.

Because many of the facts surrounding Wallace's murder remain a mystery, it is difficult to research both his life and his death; there is little consensus on many of the events from the time of his murder and from the ensuing investigation. But despite the challenges of writing such a biography, Wallace's is a worthy life to document because his story is important to many who have struggled only to find success even more trouble than the toils that paved its path. His is a story that matters to the many who have questioned our culture, to those who break society's rules. Wallace's story is important to anyone who wonders from where our children's heroes come and how their stories will end because it is those heroes who lead the future, whether in music or in other ways. His is a story that explains one facet of why American culture is what it has become, and it is important to anyone who wonders where it is going.

TIMELINE: SIGNIFICANT EVENTS IN THE LIFE OF THE NOTORIOUS B.I.G.

1972   Christopher Wallace, aka the Notorious B.I.G., is born in Brooklyn, New York, on May 21.

1989   Wallace drops out of high school to instead sell crack on the streets of Brooklyn, in his Bedford-Stuyvesant neighborhood.

1989   Wallace is arrested on a weapons charge and is sentenced to five years probation.

1991   Wallace is arrested in North Carolina for selling crack and is sentenced to nine months in jail.

1992   Wallace's demo appears in *The Source*'s "Unsigned Hype," a column read by Uptown executive Sean "Puffy" Combs.

1992   Combs and Uptown chief Andre Harrell sign Wallace to Uptown, and Wallace begins to appear on several remixes.

1993   Wallace's first child, T'Yanna Dream Wallace, is born.

1993   Wallace's single "Party and Bullshit" is released to great reviews.

1994   Wallace marries singer Faith Evans in a private ceremony in upstate New York.

1994   Wallace's first album, *Ready to Die*, hits the streets and is an instant success. The album firmly establishes Wallace as a rapper.

1994   Rapper Tupac Shakur is shot at a Manhattan studio. Shakur blames Wallace for the shooting, triggering the infamous rivalry between the West Coast's Death Row Records and the East Coast's Bad Boy Records.

1995   Wallace produces and releases Junior M.A.F.I.A.'s debut *The Conspiracy*.

1996   Tupac Shakur is killed in Las Vegas, and many allege Wallace was behind the murder.

1996   Faith Evans delivers Wallace's second child, Christopher Jordan Wallace.

1997   Wallace is shot and killed in Los Angeles, after leaving a party hosted by *Vibe* magazine. His murder remains unsolved more than a decade later.

1997   His album *Life after Death* is released posthumously, debuting at no. 1 on the Billboard 200.

1999   Bad Boy releases *Born Again*, a posthumous album that features several unreleased tracks recorded by Wallace before his death, and his single "Nasty Girl" becomes Wallace's first no. 1 Billboard hit in the United Kingdom.

2005   His family files a wrongful death suit against the City of Los Angeles, which ends in a mistrial.

2005   Bad Boy releases *Duets: The Final Chapter* to high sales and lukewarm reviews. The album, a collection of manufactured duets between Wallace and other artists, was promised to fans as the last Wallace release.

2007   Bad Boy releases *Greatest Hits*, which debuts at no. 1 on the Billboard Hot 100.

2007   Wallace's family files another wrongful death suit against the City of Los Angeles, claiming negligence on behalf of the city.

Chapter 1

GIMME THE LOOT

Christopher Wallace, better known as the Notorious B.I.G. or Biggie Smalls, lived a short life, murdered at the young age of 24. But Wallace lived those years hard and fast, experiencing an existence many could only imagine, with their only introduction to his world coming from the songs he wrote—rap lullabies that were as autobiographical as they were imaginative. Because of this, Wallace's music life started at birth, his first cry a chorus of sorts.

Christopher Wallace was born to Voletta Wallace, a single mother who worked multiple jobs to keep her small family from slipping into the hunger and poverty that gripped so many of those around them. She first came to America from Jamaica after years of seeing pictures in issues of magazines, and she envisioned a country where the blue skies shined down on the pretty, rich people in their well-decorated apartments, a country where opportunity fell with the rain. And at the young age of 19, Voletta Wallace was eager to find this new world.

After convincing the U.S. embassy in Kingston, Jamaica, that she was a designer traveling to the United States to preview fall collections, the petite Wallace moved to New York in 1968. She was 19 when she first saw the skyline of the city of which her son would one day be dubbed king.

She received a 14-day visa, one she extended before finally settling into her new American life. Although initially disappointed in New York and in America, she soon took to the city, making it her home. She took a high school equivalency test, and though she failed the first time around, she studied more and retook it, passing. Living in a rented room, she was soon able to afford a small studio on St Francis Place in Brooklyn, the borough that would become her longtime home. Wallace studied nursing at Queens College, but quickly decided that vocation was not the one for her. Transferring to Queensborough Community College, she took classes in early childhood development, a school of study that seemed natural for the smart, compassionate young woman. It was during this time that she met Selwyn at a friend's party, one of the few social outings the homebody attended. The two hit it off instantly, and Letore almost immediately became a regular fixture in her life.

A fellow Jamaican who split time between London and New York, Letore has often been described as tall man with an easy smile, fitting attributes for a small-time politician who sometimes worked as a welder. Letore was more than 20 years older than the 21-year-old Wallace, and he opened to her a world she said she had never known before. It was Letore who took Wallace to her first movie, *Shaft*, and it was with him she finally embraced the city, she later said. The two quickly fell in love. Almost as quickly, Wallace was pregnant, but when she told Letore of their upcoming child, he grew angry; it was an anger she didn't understand until a mutual friend told her Letore was married, with a family in London and a son that was almost as old as Wallace herself.

Wallace was understandably angry, though she claims to have never questioned her pregnancy, deciding instead to firmly focus on the health of her child and on her own. But she barely spoke to Letore during the rest of her pregnancy, and he happily accepted the distance, having already told her he wasn't interested in having a second family. Even when she called to have him bring her to the hospital, he didn't show up until 15 hours after she first told him she was about to have their child. But on May 21, 1972, she delivered an eight-pound boy by cesarean, a boy she named Christopher George Letore Wallace. Born with a head full of hair, Christopher Wallace was notorious around the hospital almost instantly because he was constantly active, always kicking his legs and raising a ruckus. He was also a rather large child to be born to such a petite mother—Voletta Wallace weighed only about 120 pounds at her son's birth. She wasn't allowed to hold her son until he was days old, given that she was sick with a contagious infection from the cesarean incision.

BROOKLYN BOY

Less than two weeks after Christopher Wallace's birth, the mother and son moved into a large, three-bedroom apartment in a Brooklyn brownstone on St. James Street, situated between the notorious Bedford-Stuyvesant and affluent Clinton Hill neighborhoods. They lived blocks from a methadone clinic, a few feet from dealers and addicts, and a breath away from the streets that claimed so many young men.

A neighborhood marked by unemployment and limited options, the streets of Bedford-Stuyvesant spawned many notable rappers, including Busta Rhymes, Aaliyah, Jay-Z, Talib Kweli, Mos Def, Big Daddy Kane, the GZA, and members of the Junior M.A.F.I.A., including Lil' Kim. The area has been directly impacted by many of the social changes throughout history, from the white flight of the 1950s to the racial riots of the 1960s to the crack epidemic of the early 1980s to the gentrification of the early 1990s, a trend that continues today. The neighborhood, though originally mostly white, became almost all black in the early 1960s, a trend that has reversed as its spacious brownstones have become attractive to many whites wanting out of the cramped, expensive Manhattan. Still, though, the neighborhood boasts a 70 percent black population, and although gentrification continues to creep into its blocks, the neighborhood is much the same as it was when Voletta Wallace first moved there with her young son Christopher.

The young, single mother worked full-time while attending school and taking care of her son. By the time Christopher was two, Letore had quit coming around altogether, and Voletta Wallace took full care of her son, whom she nicknamed Chrissy Pooh because of his love of Winnie the Pooh stories. She said she doted on her Christopher, giving him everything he wanted, including plenty of food.

"The name Biggie, he earned that," Voletta Wallace wrote in her book about her son. "During that time, the mindset was that the bigger the child, the healthier and happier he or she is" (Wallace and McKenzie, 2005, p. 51).

A young Christopher Wallace always drank whole milk (never skim), ate burgers instead of vegetables, snacked often, and always cleaned his plate. From childhood on, his favorite meal was waffles topped with ice cream and a side of bacon, a meal that easily added to his already bulky size.

Past that, though, Voletta Wallace used her growing experience in early childhood development to teach Christopher to read and write far earlier than any of his playmates. And just as he was advanced in his studies, he also surpassed the other children in size. Once he turned five, Wallace was much larger than the other children his age, though he reportedly never used his size to intimidate others. Instead, he opted for charm, evoking the same appeal he carried until his death.

Voletta Wallace worked extra hours to pay for private school once her son was of school age, enrolling him at St. Peter Claver Elementary, a nearby private Catholic school. Nicknamed Captain Chris, the young Wallace made many friends, including Michael "Master Mike" Bynum and "Heartbroken" Hubert Sams, two boys he considered his best friends. These were Wallace's first real male companions, given that he was raised an only child by a single mother.

Living in a poor, violent neighborhood but attending a private school marked by uniforms, the boys became used to fighting for even the simplest of things. Eventually, Wallace formed a small "protection" group called The Hawks, which was no more than the three boys protecting each other by each carrying around small weapons most sources say they actually never used. Wallace even wrote a small rap for the group: "Heartbroken Hubert, Captain Chris and Master Mike / . . . Why's everybody always picking on us?"

But Voletta Wallace never knew of his troubles on the street. She was strict with Christopher, not allowing him to play with many of the neighborhood kids and instead choosing to stock the house with food, music, and video games to keep Christopher home. He would often invite friends up to his apartment, almost always having more stuff than they did in their homes. One of these friends was Chico Delvac, a young boy who knew all the street characters Wallace wanted to know. With Chico, Wallace first explored music, listening to the Fat Boys and Run D.M.C. And it was with Chico that Wallace left his apartment to explore the streets below, an exploration undertaken only while his mother was working or at school pursuing her master's in early childhood education.

When he was 10, the young Wallace fell off a city bus, an accident later determined to be the fault of the driver. The city later settled with the family for an undisclosed five-figure amount, most of which Voletta Wallace put into a savings fund for her son. But he was laid up for six months, and Wallace, already a hefty boy, gained even more weight while his leg healed. Once better, though, he began to sneak out while his mother was at work or at school, spending time down at the corner with Chico, where he met many of the people he'd only seen before in passing.

HITTING THE STREETS

"When she would go to work or to school, I'd be all over the place," Wallace told *Vibe* reporter Cheo Hodari Coker. "I'd be outside . . . smoking cigarettes and drinking Calvin Coolers. Just doing shit that I knew I wasn't supposed to do" (Coker, 2003, p. 21).

He spent most of his time on Fulton Avenue, just a block up from his house. There he was first introduced to the street from which his mother had tried so hard to shield him, the one filled with dealers, drunks, and men throwing dice. And even though he was smart, with a talent for drawing, this was the life to which he was most attracted. This was the existence he most sought.

Although Wallace made some money bagging groceries at the local Met Foods, he still didn't have what he wanted: new clothes, new shoes, jewelry, and all the things he saw down at the corner. Having to ask his mom for extra money didn't fit into the image he wanted so much to be his.

First enrolled at the private Queen of All Saints School, Christopher Wallace soon decided that the life of a Catholic school boy was no longer for him, and he demanded to be transferred to the public Westinghouse High School, a typical inner-city school where the students ran the classroom, wars were fought on the playground, and police were more likely than the principle to discipline the students. There Wallace attended class alongside Shawn "Jay-Z" Carter and Trevor "Busta Rhymes" Smith, two young men that would go on to be as big of stars as Wallace was meant to be.

Once in public school, Wallace was as good as gone, with his desire to be a part of the streets stronger than ever before. To him, drugs offered more money and more opportunity than school ever would, along with the freedom he always wanted. Even the freedom he found at a public school wasn't enough, and before long, he considered dropping out, choosing the education of the streets over that of a classroom. Wallace knew he could make the cash he wanted slinging crack, an option that became increasingly appealing.

THE RISE OF CRACK

Once considered a drug only for rich white people, cocaine found its popularity during the disco days of the 1970s, a trend that continued into the early 1980s. But many couldn't afford the drug, and as its market aged, it became less fashionable to do the pricey powder. Still, though, huge supplies flooded the Caribbean islands as dealers in countries such as Columbia continued to manufacture huge amounts of the drug. But with the supply far outweighing the demand, prices dropped by up to 80 percent in the United States.

Soon, though, someone thought to mix cocaine with baking powder, creating a substance originally called base. In South and Central America, use of base became more common, and before long, this form of cocaine was introduced to the United States.

First reports of what we now call crack cocaine came from San Diego, Houston, and Miami, though the drug didn't reach mainstream prominence until 1980, when Richard Pryor set himself afire while freebasing, or smoking cocaine. The comic reportedly went on a 72-hour smoking binge that ended in an explosion caused by the ether he used to smoke the cocaine. According to an article in the *New York Times*, Pryor was found more than a mile from his Los Angeles home, in shock. He had third-degree burns all over the top half his body and was hospitalized for nearly two months as doctors performed a series of skin grafts meant to repair his body. The incident brought widespread attention to this new form of drug use, bringing cocaine even closer to the black man.

Notably safer than freebasing, making crack does not require flammable chemicals, and its preparation is simple yet powerful. A mixture of water and either baking soda or ammonia is combined with powder cocaine, and this is then boiled to remove its solid parts, which are then cooled and cut into small bits, often called rocks. Easy and quick, the preparation of crack allows for dealers to maximize even the smallest amounts of cocaine, resulting in fast returns for dealers and even faster highs for its users.

Many have been blamed for the spread of crack across America, with most news articles focusing on two men, Oscar Danilo Blandon and Ricky Ross (U.S. Department of Justice, 1997). Both were based in Los Angeles, though their operations spread across the country. Taking advantage of the effortless nature of crack—highly addictive, easily made, and readily accessible—dealers who once sold higher-end products such as heroin turned to the new drug, helping its spread to the depths of inner-city neighborhoods. Some dealers stepped up to help create pipelines between cities, such as Brian "Waterhead Bo" Bennett, who was largely responsible for the East Coast–West Coast crack channel between Los Angeles and Washington, D.C. Massive amounts of the drug moved between the two cities, with more than an estimated 2,000 pounds of crack passing through Bennett's hands each week. Eventually, though, he was busted, taking down with him the infamous Michael "Harry O" Harris, a notorious drug kingpin whose operations spread across the country, with firm roots in at least 11 states. Harris was firmly connected to the Bloods, though he often worked directly with Columbia drug lords (U.S. Department of Justice, 1997).

Harris was also heavily involved in the entertainment industry and had been one of the first black men to produce a Broadway play, a feat he had achieved through *Checkmates*, which had starred a then-unknown Denzel Washington. Both Harris and Bennett were represented by David Kenner, a lawyer known for his high-profile clients as well as his attitude inside the courtroom: cool and calm as he confidently defended his clients.

The crack epidemic—generally considered to have occurred between 1984 and 1990—devastated parts of most major U.S. cities, especially New York, Houston, Los Angeles, and Atlanta. Even in smaller cities like Savannah, dealers clung to the corners of housing projects and surrounding neighborhoods, offering up small packets of crack to most anyone driving by. In Boston, homicide rates soared alongside drug use, and entire neighborhoods were swallowed whole by the epidemic as dealers took the street in direct defiance of authorities. Under the bright sun of San Diego came the discreet deals, outstretched palms appearing to shake when instead they were passing cash for crack, with both dealer and user quickly pulling away, looking away as if the exchange had never happened.

From his window on St. James Place, Wallace saw such deals happen daily, and he soon longed for that sort of underground existence. He saw Chico, a kid his own age, wearing the sort of clothes he dreamed of wearing, Chico's fingers adorned with the rings Wallace longed to wear. He wanted to be down with the streets. He wanted to be a hustler.

"I heard about crack on the news and I was like, 'That's what niggas must be doing,'" Wallace once told a reporter (Coker, 2003, p. 31).

Soon Chico invited Wallace to nearby Fulton Street, just a block away from where Wallace lived with his mom. Wallace was introduced to several other dealers, and he realized how high the stakes could get. At any point, an undercover cop could bust you, a rival gang member could shoot you, or a thug could steal your stash or cash. And although Wallace was at first scared of those possibilities, he soon found that his desire for money outweighed any fear, and he learned the way of the street.

LIFE AS A HUSTLER

At first selling marijuana, Wallace soon discovered the fast cash of crack, a drug that was as easy to sell as it was to make and that didn't require a dealer to have too many connections in order to be successful. Because of this, Wallace was able to slip in quickly and swiftly, at first working with others on small deals and then stepping up fairly quickly to larger deals with repeat customers.

At home, his mother still reigned, and most of Wallace's friends still feared her. He continued to live a double life, hiding things he bought with drug money on the roof of their apartment building. He still wore the clothes his mom had purchased for him, changing into his new clothes after she left for work, though he was careful to put back on the clothes she had bought before she returned home, keeping up the guise of a poor teenager with no income. His mother had little clue of his new life, even when it stared her in the face. She once told a reporter that she had thought crack vials she had sometimes found in his room were perfume bottles. Another time, she discovered drying crack on a plate. Thinking they were mashed potatoes, she threw the drugs out. Later Wallace and a friend sifted through the trash trying the find the drugs, which held a high street value. Once they finally found them, they had to clean off hot wing sauce and other debris in order to sell the valuable drug.

Despite being an honor roll student, Wallace finally decided to quit school at just 16, during his junior year of high school, deciding that he wouldn't go to college or to art school, as he had always thought he might. Although he was a smart, talented artist, he saw his future only in drugs. He was chasing the cash and wanted the valuable daytime hours to sell to people cashing their welfare checks in the morning or trading their food stamps for change.

According to her biography, his mother was concerned that he wasn't in school and was instead spending his time on the streets. Because of this she filed a PINS, or person in need of supervision, warrant and had to spend an entire day in court to get judicial approval. "I felt like a criminal. That made me so angry that I left that courthouse in tears, that I had to go through all of that just to get him off the streets" (Wallace and McKenzie, 2005, p. 67). Finally after many days, Christopher called his mom. The police were looking for him, and she told him he could either go back to school or not return to her house. He at first chose school, though that only lasted a short while before he finally quit again, as he had a few weeks earlier. Soon he was on the streets, occasionally selling drugs and often hanging out with other neighborhood kids, some of whom would later become Junior M.A.F.I.A.

Once a full-time dealer, though, he realized that a life slinging crack wasn't as easy as he had thought it would be and that the cash didn't always flow. Some weeks, he'd make only a few hundred dollars; other weeks, a few thousand. He later claimed to make anywhere from $1,200 to $1,500 a day and boasted of selling of drugs to anyone, including pregnant women.

"We used to have this rule that was, 'We ain't serving to no pregnant ladies,'" Wallace once told a reporter. "And there was a pregnant lady who used to come see us every day from Jersey...I'm like...if I don't give it to her, someone else will" (Coker, 2003, p. 39).

Wallace also often camped outside check-cashing shops early each morning, knowing that many would be hungry for drugs as soon as they had their cash in hand. But despite his efforts to be tough, Wallace was known around the town as nice and not much of a danger, despite what he later said on his album *Ready to Die*. On it, he rapped about hard times on the street. But at his local hangouts, such as Brother Mike's Barber Shop, Wallace and his friends would smoke weed while drinking what was later called Thug's Passion, a potent mixture of Alizé liquor and Hennessey cognac. He'd throw dice with friends and hit on pretty ladies. At home, his mother still made him dinner and told him what a great kid he was.

In 1990, while holding court at a local corner, Wallace was arrested alongside several friends; though he didn't have drugs on him at the time, he did have a loaded, unregistered gun. Because Wallace was 17 and without any previous offenses, a judge sentenced him to only five years probation. Around this time, several officers came by Wallace's house and told Voletta Wallace her son was dealing drugs. She refused to accept what they were saying, vehemently denying their accusations, reportedly replying, "Not my Christopher." She believed in her son, despite his having dropped out of high school and despite the recent gun charge. She felt sure there was no way he'd sell drugs. But when she told him of the officers' visit later, he finally came clean, admitting to her that the police were telling the truth. She kicked him out of the house for two weeks after taking out a life insurance policy on him, saying that if he was selling drugs, he was as good as dead.

Around this time, Wallace realized how much money was to be had down South, especially in North and South Carolina, where an old friend named Robert "Zauqael" Cagle ran a rather profitable business. It was in a Raleigh-area Days Inn that the two watched *Let's Do It Again*, a comedy starring Bill Cosby and Poitier. Actor Calvin Lockhart played a character named Biggie Smalls. Knowing his friend rapped, Cagle reportedly turned to Wallace, suggesting he add on "Smalls" to his nickname "Biggie," which he sometimes used while rapping. Wallace instantly took on "Smalls," and a few nights later, he performed under that name at a local nightclub's open mic night. Wallace reportedly drove the crowd wild with his freestyle. It was his first time ever on stage.

His business in Raleigh expanded, and eventually he and Zauqael rented a three-bedroom house just inside town. But as their scope expanded, so did police scrutiny, and Wallace was soon busted and jailed, his bail set at $25,000. With no options, he called his mom back in Brooklyn. Voletta Wallace had saved almost all the money the younger Wallace had received after being hit by the city bus when he was just 13, and because the money was technically his, she helped by sending the cash needed to make bail. He immediately returned home, though he later was sentenced and served nine months in state prison.

Once released and back in Brooklyn, Wallace stayed at a friend's house, still selling drugs on the streets of Bedford-Stuyvesant. Even after his mother let him back into the house, he took to the streets each day, becoming a central figure in the local drug scene, where he was called Big Chris. As his reign over the blocks continued, some dubbed him the Mayor of St. James, a title he accepted with pride.

THE PIVOTAL MIX TAPE

But it wasn't all drugs and drinking. Chico and Wallace liked to listen to music on Wallace's boom box, buying cheap mix tapes sold on the corner of their neighborhood. Although Wallace loved LL Cool J and some of the other prominent rappers of the time, he began to dig a new style, one that spoke to the way he lived his life, a style called gangsta rap.

Emerging out of California in the late 1980s, the first strains of gangsta rap were heard in N.W.A.'s *Straight Outta Compton*, an album—and style—that took immediate hold of the rap audience's attention. Marked by violent lyrics over soul and funk beats, gangsta rap tends to lyrically focus on women, drugs, and gang violence, often with a particular group pledging allegiance to a particular gang, be it the Crips or the Bloods.

Wallace immediately took to this new style, later claiming that it inspired him to continue rapping on his own. Sometimes he and some friends, including Damien "D-Roc" Butler, would hang out with the Old Gold Brothers and DJ 50 Grand, a local turntablist. They would hole up in Wallace's bedroom, listening to mix tapes and albums and smoking copious amounts of marijuana. One day they went over to 50 Grand's house and made their way down to his basement, where Wallace saw his two turntables, a mixer, a microphone, and a huge stack of records.

Wallace told 50 Grand that he had musical skills and that he knew his way around a microphone. According to an interview Wallace later gave a *Vibe* reporter, 50 Grand then stepped behind the turntables, grabbed two copies of *Ultimate Breaks and Beats, Volume 24*, and put both records on the turntables. He chose the fourth track, the Emotions' "Blind Alley," a track that had previously served as background for a Big Daddy Kane song.

Wallace grabbed the microphone and set to rhyming, his style slow but methodical, his voice low but hypnotizing. Everyone was transfixed, and when he ended along with the track, 50 said, "Let's make a tape."

The scene repeated, although this time it was caught on cassette. Though Wallace had only played around with emceeing before, he had always thought that he had skills and that he could rap if he wanted. Hearing his voice play back on tape proved it.

And he wasn't the only one who thought so. 50 Grand was amazed at the skills of this overweight dealer standing in his basement. He immediately took the tape to his friend Mister Cee, a DJ and producer who worked the turntables for Big Daddy Kane. When 50 handed over the mix tape, Mister Cee was leaving on tour with Kane, but promised to listen to it when he returned. The very day he got back, September 23, 1991, 50 knocked on his door, insisting Mister Cee listen to the tape then and there. He did.

"I always felt like it was just inevitable for me to have heard that tape, because of all the things that was involved in it," Mister Cee later told a reporter. "Bed-Stuy Brooklyn. Rhymin' over the 'Blind Alley.' It was a message from God that I had to hear that tape" (Coker, 2003, p. 53).

Cee asked 50 and Wallace to rerecord the tape, cleaning it up some so that he could present it to some of his industry friends. Using equipment he had at the house, Cee caught Wallace on tape once more. It was even better than before.

Cee passed the tape along to old friend Matteo Capoluongo, known professionally as Matty C, a local writer who penned the popular and influential column "Unsigned Hype" in *The Source*. Artists receiving favorable reviews often scored record contracts because artist and repertoire (A&R) representatives often scoured the column, looking for new talent. One such rep was a young man from Harlem, a smart, educated 20-year-old who scoured the pages of magazines, looking for the next act to sign to Uptown Records, the label where he worked. He read Matty C's review in *The Source* and instantly picked up the phone, inviting the writer over to his office. There he heard the tape himself and began pounding Matty C with questions.

"What does he look like?" he reportedly asked. Matty paused for a moment before telling music representative Sean Combs that Wallace was a dark-skinned, rather overweight man with a lazy eye. Combs, ever the marketer, began thinking right away of how he could sell this new rapper to the general public.

Chapter 2

ALL ABOUT THE BENJAMINS

Almost as soon as Combs heard Wallace's rhymes, he sent word that he wanted to meet the rapper. Along with Mister Cee, Wallace went to Combs's office at Uptown Records, where Combs worked as an A&R representative. Started by Andre Harrell in the late 1980s, Uptown had on its roster Heavy D, a rapper whose rhymes were more commercial than they were hardcore, as well as singer Mary J. Blige and quartet Jodeci. Having first started in music as half of the rap duo Dr. Jeckyll and Mr. Hyde, Harrell worked as an assistant to his friend Russell Simmons, who, with Rick Rubin, started Def Jam Records, the first huge hip-hop label. Def Jam brought Beastie Boys and LL Cool J to national audiences, and the success of those two albums helped the label secure a distribution deal with Columbia/CBS Records. From there the label went on to sign some of the biggest hip-hop heavies, bringing to the mainstream a sound most people had never heard before, a sound that represented the streets of New York and its boroughs.

But Harrell envisioned a different sound, one he sometimes described as sexy while also classic. Although traditional R&B no longer held the strong appeal it once had, Harrell—along with those he employed—helped bring to the mainstream a sound that was new to many: a grittier, more hip-hop version with R&B stylings.

Combs fit well into this image and was only 20 when he first took an internship at the label, one secured by Heavy D. The two had grown up in the same hometown—Mount Vernon—and Heavy introduced Combs to Harrell, who offered Combs an unpaid position. A student at Howard University in Washington, D.C., Combs boarded a train each morning at 5 A.M. to arrive in New York at 10 A.M., where he promptly reported to work.

To Combs, this job represented his future, and always ambitious, he did all he could to impress his new boss. Eventually, he moved in with Harrell, renting a room in the record executive's spacious New Jersey house. There he met many of the industry's leaders and made many of the connections that helped him become the mogul he is today. Harrell became his mentor and helped the young man through several situations, including a 1991 concert he promoted that soon proved deadly.

Wanting to promote HIV awareness as well as support Uptown artists, Combs planned a concert with headliner Heavy D to be held at the City College of New York gymnasium. With the concert vastly oversold and tremendously overcrowded, Combs had several of his doormen lock the only door to the only emergency exit, putting a table in front of it. As tickets outside were continually sold, despite the overcrowding, people inside began demanding to leave as people outside tried desperately to get into the gym. Soon, chaos erupted, and a stampede followed. Glass doors were broken into bits, and bedlam broke out, spurring the frantic crowd even more. After the dust settled, nine people were dead, including a good friend of Combs. Courts later determined that Combs and Heavy D were partially responsible for the deaths, as was the City College of New York, which had left security up to Combs, despite knowing the event was oversold.

Harrell rushed back from a vacation in Barbados to help the young Combs in any way. But because criminal charges were never filed, Comb escaped any notable problems, past any emotional issues he carried with him from having left the situation literally with blood on his hands. Combs still weighed heavily in on the label's daily workings, interacting with the artists as much as possible. He changed Jodeci from country boys from Charlotte, North Carolina, to sexy city men and was responsible for many of the label's top remixes; he had a strong ear for new, solid talent. When Uptown A&R representative Kurt Woodley quit, Combs asked for his job, telling Harrell that not only was he the future of the label; he was the future audience as well. Harrell listened and hired the young man. Once in position, Combs signed Mary J. Blige, a singer who would one day be crowned the "queen of hip-hop soul" by numerous publications and people in the music industry.

And although Combs liked his new artist, he also wanted to move in a new direction, one that was more hardcore, more real for him. When he heard Wallace's demo, he knew he had found what he'd been looking for.

Just a few days after Combs first heard that fateful demo, Mister Cee and Wallace came to Combs's office, ready to talk business. Put off by

Wallace's seemingly shy demeanor, Combs asked Wallace to kick a rhyme, and Wallace did. Combs was entranced, and once Wallace stopped, Combs instantly offered him a record deal. But before Wallace could sign any contracts, he had to meet Andre Harrell, whose old-school sensibilities had him wanting someone attractive, someone the ladies would find sexy. Within a month, the four met at Sylvia's, a soul food restaurant on 125th street. Though Harrell liked Wallace's demo, he wasn't quite sure the big man could fit on their label. Wallace was unusually quiet, not speaking, not eating. After a rather unimpressive meeting, the group stepped into Harrell's black Lincoln Town Car, headed back to the Uptown headquarters. On the way, Harrell asked Wallace to rhyme. Mister Cee was ready and had a cassette on hand to supply a beat. He put it into the car's deck. A beat filled the car, and Wallace started rapping.

Almost as soon as he was finished, Harrell offered him a contract, wanting him to immediately start work with the popular label. Combs still put Wallace in the studio, where he recorded one unreleased track called "Biggie Got the Hype Shit," a danceable track featuring a boisterous Wallace, whose excitement at being in the studio is evident in both his compelling tone and his energetic delivery. Considered a test to see how Wallace would fare in a studio, the track was produced by Mister Cee along with Jesse West, with heavily sampling from James Brown's hit "I Got to Move." The song was considered the first real example of what would become classic Wallace style, and it has been described by the few who heard it as a masterful mix of both the crude and the ingenious. Chances of it being released were destroyed, though, when the master tapes burned in a fire at the New York studio where it was recorded.

One of Wallace's first appearances was on Heavy D's "A Buncha Niggas," a pop-rap song that also featured Busta Rhymes, 3rd Eye, Guru, and Rob-o. Easily forgettable, the song features Wallace's rhymes against a vocal backing of several men asking, "Who's on the microphone? / A buncha niggas!" Wallace also appeared on Neneh Cherry's "Buddy X," one of her last hits before fading into obscurity. A Lenny Kravitz diss track, the song featured a toned-down Wallace weighing in with several lines about the trappings of relationships, taking the narrative tone listeners would soon know well. But perhaps the most famous of his appearances was on Mary J. Blige's "Real Love," which sampled Betty Wright's 1972 single "Clean Up Woman." The song not only helped sell Mary J. Blige's *What's the 411?* but also placed Wallace in the national spotlight. Shortly after, he appeared on "Dolly My Baby," a single by Jamaican dancehall artist Super Cat. It was this appearance that solidified his role as an artist not only at Uptown but also in his mother's eyes.

Early one morning, Voletta Wallace was listening to one of her usual stations when she became increasingly annoyed by its static. Turning the dial, she finally settled on a channel playing Toni Braxton's "Breathe Again." Soon, though, the song ended, and a rap song began. As she reached for the dial, she heard a familiar voice, one that sounded much like her son. At the end of the song, the DJ said, "That was Super Cat with Biggie Smalls." Right after the identification was popular female rapper Da Brat asking, "How you living, Biggie Smalls?" It was early in the morning, about 5 A.M., and Voletta's son Christopher was still asleep. His voice came on again, and she got up from bed and went to his room, waking him up to ask if he knew someone named Super Cat, or Da Brat, and if he had a song on the radio. He said yes before drifting back to sleep, leaving his mother gaping in the doorway.

Despite hearing all the music that had come from his room over the years, his mother had no idea that his claims of being a rapper could, in any way, be true. It wasn't that she didn't believe what her son told her, she said, but instead that she did not realize that music was this important to him and that he would actually be on the radio. Besides that, he still lived in her house rent-free and ate food she bought, a lifestyle she didn't usually associate with professional musicians.

Even though he had worked on several high-profile songs, he was still broke. The album originally promised seemed slow in coming, and he appeared only on others' works and had nothing of his own. And now, more than ever, he needed some cash. He had just found out that Jan Jackson, a neighborhood girl, was pregnant with his child.

One of Wallace's first real girlfriends, Jackson was a girl from his neighborhood and almost could have been Wallace's sister, given how much the two looked alike—both overweight with dark charcoal skin—but they were also similarly minded, having almost the same sense of humor anchored by the reality that comes from having spent time on the streets. The couple had split up at some point for a time, but the child was his. He was still waiting for that record deal to come through, but because the money was slow in coming, and he had a child on the way, he decided to go back to the streets and start hustling again.

Wallace still had many of the same connections as before, and although there was plenty of money to be made in Brooklyn, there was even more to be made down in North Carolina, where addicts would travel up to 50 miles to get crack cocaine. He made the trek and soon, according to some estimates, was pulling in tens of thousands hustling. But amid the frantic calls from addicts coming through on Wallace's pager were calls from

Combs in New York. Finally, on a Sunday, Wallace returned his page and learned that his record deal had finally come through and that he had an advance waiting for him back in New York. He could have taken his time to return to New York, pulling in that one last hustle before it was time to go legitimate. But something inside Wallace told him it was time to return north.

He left Monday morning, headed straight for New York City. That night, back in Raleigh, police raided the house where he had been staying, arresting everyone inside. To Wallace, this was a sign that he was, in fact, just where he needed to be: off the streets, not hustling and instead earning a legitimate living through music.

His advance was cheap—approximately $125,000—and was supposed to cover all recording costs as well as any other expenses he incurred. Still, to Wallace, being paid to write and perform was better than any payday on the streets, and as soon as he returned home, he set up shop in his bedroom and began to work.

Already following in his friend Wallace's footsteps, neighborhood boy Lil' Cease had quit school at 15 and taken to hustling on Fulton Street. But Wallace, believing in Cease's potential, pulled him into his scene, enlisting the young man as an assistant of sorts while Wallace wrote inside his bedroom, the room that would later be referred to as the one-room shack in his song "Juicy." In those days, Voletta Wallace was still the law of the land, and any visitor, no matter who he was, had to obey her rules. Shoelaces had to be tied, feet were not allowed on the coffee table, and hats weren't to be worn inside. "Yes, ma'am" and "no, ma'am" were always said, and no one ever addressed her with their mouths full or in any sort of disrespectful tone.

It was in that "one-room shack" Wallace penned what was to become his first hit single, a song whose name came from the lyrics of revolutionary poets though, in true Wallace fashion, he easily made the phrase his own.

"PARTY AND BULLSHIT"

Produced by Easy Mo Bee, Wallace's hit single "Party and Bullshit" first appeared on the soundtrack for the forgettable 1993 comedy thriller *Who's the Man*. Light yet strong, the song reflects the lyricist Wallace had become, and in it he delivers clever lines in his trademark charismatic and controlling manner.

The song features Wallace as the narrator, with Mo Bee's beats use of organs and strings sampled heavily from ESG's classic song "UFO." The song has been remixed twice: in a jazz version by Bronx producer and DJ Lord Finesse and in a Combs-heavy version called "Puffy's Remix."

The title for the single comes from the Last Poets' song "When the Revolution Comes," in which the phrase "party and bullshit" is repeated several times. The Last Poets—musicians from Civil Rights–era Harlem— are often considered to have heavily shaped modern rap and have been called the godfathers of the style. Throughout the years, they have collaborated with a variety of musicians, including Wu-Tang Clan's Black Market Militia (on "The Final Call") and Common (on "The Corner").

Easy Mo Bee was the last producer to work with Miles Davis, having produced his studio album *Doo-Bop* in 1992, winning a Grammy for that effort. Bee was also from Bedford-Stuyvesant, having lived his whole life in the neighborhood and having known Wallace from the streets. Bee, also known as Osten Harvey Jr., grew up with Big Daddy Kane and often worked with the popular artist, most notably on his hit "It's a Big Daddy Thing." Bee also produced most of the GZA's critically acclaimed *Words from the Genius* and worked with a variety of rappers, including Tupac Shakur for his pivotal release *Me against the World*.

Just after the single hit the street, Wallace and old friend Damien "D-Roc" Butler were walking in their neighborhood, just after having dinner at Butler's grandmother's house. Joking around, the two talked about the future and how they would spend the money once it started flowing. Soon, though, they heard sirens, and within seconds, the police were on them. Wallace had in his pockets an unregistered gun, which he immediately threw out into a nearby yard. One officer retrieved the gun while another overtook the two, arresting them. There were two men and one gun—someone had to take responsibility. In the interrogation room at Brooklyn's 79th precinct, the arresting officer told the two to make a decision as to who would take responsibility, leaving the old friends to discuss it. Wallace had a child on the way, a single on the charts, and a recording deal. Add in several prior arrests for weapons, as well as a current probation for weapons-related charge, and it was clear Wallace would serve several years if convicted. Butler shouldered the blame, telling officers the gun was his. He was convicted and sentenced to four years, though he didn't serve his full sentence.

Almost as soon as Butler was hauled off to jail, Wallace's life suffered another setback. His mother, always the beacon of strength, was sick. Tests showed she had breast cancer, and although it was in the beginning stages, she needed almost all the lymph nodes surrounding her breast removed, to prevent the disease's rampant spread. She didn't require chemotherapy, but the surgery left her weak, forcing a slow recovery witnessed by her son.

During this time, he actively wrote, penning what would later become the core of his debut album, *Ready to Die*, a force of hip-hop many consider to have permanently changed hip-hop.

WELCOME TO DEATH ROW

Without a doubt, the rap industry had already significantly changed over the past few years, most notably because of a small label hailing from Compton, California, and a man named Suge.

Standing at a formidable 6 feet 3 inches and weighing more than 350 pounds, Marion "Suge" Knight was nothing less than intimidating. Originally from Compton, Knight had moved to Las Vegas after taking a place on the University of Las Vegas football team, a team notorious for its after-school activities, which included petty drug sales and part-time jobs running the doors at local clubs. Knight left college during his senior year to join the Los Angeles Rams in 1987, during a player strike. The team needed players to fill in the gaps left by the regular players, and Knight, a solid player, easily fit the bill. But almost as soon as the strike ended, Knight was permanently benched, and before long, he officially left the team. Within short time, he was arrested after attacking a man in what was later determined to be an auto theft. Charged with attempted murder, grand larceny of an auto, and the use of a deadly weapon to commit a crime, Knight was given only probation and a fine, and he decided to move back to California, back to Compton and to his family.

Having relocated to the poverty-stricken area from Mississippi to escape racism and to be closer to family, Knight's parents—a teacher and a custodian—had raised Knight in a comfortable home. Nicknamed "Sugar Bear" as a child, Knight was always an athlete, offering him the only allowable excuse to sidestep gang membership. Even so, he carried close friendships with many gang members, most notably the Tree Top Pirus, a Bloods-affiliated gang that ran rampant in his neighborhood. Many of the gang members were proud of Knight for being a good football player, and he enjoyed a certain level of respect among the Pirus usually reserved for other gang members. When he left the Rams and returned to Compton, he rekindled those friendships, using the old connections to sell cocaine and guns. Knight also secured work as a bodyguard for Bobby Brown, who was then enjoying the success of his top-selling album *Don't Be Cruel*, as well as his recent Grammy win for the single "Every Little Step." Through Brown, Knight made many connections, including one that would go on to shape the music industry, his connection with Tracy Lynn Curtis, better known as the D.O.C.

Originally from Texas, the D.O.C. was part of the Fila Fresh Crew, through which he first met Dr. Dre after working as a DJ during some performances of Dre's first group, the World Class Wreckin' Cru. The World Class Wreckin' Cru was later included on the N.W.A. and the Posse compilation released in 1987. Not long after, D.O.C. moved to Compton to work more closely with N.W.A., filling in for Ice Cube when he temporarily relocated to Arizona for an architecture course. Dre later produced the D.O.C.'s debut album *No One Can Do It Better*. He also is reported to have written most of *Efil4zaggin*, N.W.A.'s second album, released by the newly formed Ruthless Records. But as N.W.A. became more successful, and as their album sales and tour revenue increased, and manager Jerry Heller was brought in, some members—especially Dr. Dre and Ice Cube—began to question Eazy-E and his money management, doubting that Eazy and Heller were being fair in their practices. Ice Cube, who wrote most of the songs, received only $32,700 for his work on two albums that had combined sales of $3 million and received barely any money from a tour that earned approximately $650,000 (Ro, 1999, p. 44).

With album sales for his Ruthless release *No One Could Do It Better* hitting platinum status, the D.O.C. was on top of the world, having received a top rating from the well-respected magazine *The Source* as well as the opportunity to continue working as a successful solo artist. But his good fortune wouldn't last long. At the height of his album's popularity, the D.O.C. was in a terrible accident. His face needed more than 20 reconstructive surgeries, and his larynx was crushed. His voice was gone.

Knight kept vigil at the hospital and drove D.O.C.'s mom back and forth to the hospital, becoming close with their family. Both Eazy and Heller kept their distance from the hospital, something of which Knight reminded the D.O.C. regularly as the two discussed the artist's future (Ro, 1998, p. 44). To Knight, the answer was clear. The D.O.C. had valuable experience in the music industry, having worked as a performer himself. With Knight's backing, the two could form their own record label, righting many of the wrongs Knight felt companies like Ruthless often committed.

Cube was increasingly unhappy with N.W.A. and called to order a band meeting to discuss both finances and the future. Eazy didn't show, and almost immediately, Ice Cube left the band, headed for New York to pursue a solo career. D.O.C. told Dre that Knight was looking over his own contracts and that Knight would be happy to review the contracts for Dre as well as his girlfriend, singer Michel'le. In one of their many conversations, D.O.C. told Knight how Ice Cube and Dre felt shafted. Knight offered to talk to Dre and to see whether there was a way he could help. D.O.C.

set up a meeting, and soon Dre and Knight met in what was easily one of the most pivotal moments in rap history. Dre also wanted to leave Ruthless but felt tied to the label, largely in part because of his contract with Heller and Eazy as well as Sony, who distributed Ruthless' releases. Knight offered to get him out of the obligation if Dre would possibly want to work together by starting their own label, becoming partners. Dre agreed, and Knight visited Heller in what would later be described as a violent confrontation, one in which Heller has always claimed Knight repeatedly threatened him with violence. According to reports, Heller bought several guns and became increasingly paranoid after the incident (Ro, 1999, pp. 44–45, 49–52).

D.O.C. was also old friends with Mario Lavelle Johnson, better known as Chocolate, who was also from Dallas but had come to Los Angeles with friend DJ Tee-Low. By the time the two arrived and while he was negotiating Dre's release from Ruthless Records, Knight had started a label called Funky Enough Records along with D.O.C. and Tom Kline, a sports agent whom Knight protected. Kline let Knight used his Beverly Hills office as the headquarters for the label, and Knight offered Kline part of the company in return. Knight wanted to sign Chocolate, as well as the popular artist DJ Quik. Though he didn't offer any money, Knight gave his artists certain perks, like a place to live and plane tickets home when they wanted to see family. In return, Knight received the artists' loyalty because he was one of them, having also grown in the 'hood. Because rap was becoming a multimillion-dollar industry, the pressure to appeal to wider audiences could be overwhelming. Many considered Knight to be a music executive who didn't succumb to the pressure to "cross over" into white audience by forsaking edge and who offered to his artists promises about sticking to ideals of making true black music while at the same time being paid for it (Ro, 1999, pp. 31–32).

Knight also stepped up as a "protector" of other musicians, including Mary J. Blige and Jodeci, who were still at Uptown. Through some of his sources, Knight had heard their contracts were unfair, and he unexpectedly showed up at the Uptown offices to talk to label head Andre Harrell. Though Harrell has never actively discussed what happened in his offices, he did offer both Mary J. Blige and Jodeci more money, and he has always maintained that Knight did not threaten him, though he did soon staff armed guards at his shows. Knight also once showed up at one of Wallace's recording sessions while they were finishing *Ready to Die*, and he posed for pictures with both Combs and Wallace. Combs later said Knight simply stood at the back of the studio, his arms crossed, watching the process and not saying much to anyone there.

But just as suddenly as the label started, Tom Kline backed out his deal with Knight, kicking the small label out of his Beverly Hills office and denying any more funding. Knight held onto Chocolate's master tapes, but looked toward a new venture, one in which he'd hold all the power as to not have someone like Tom Kline shut things down again.

Soon a man Knight once protected introduced him to Dick Griffey, the head of SOLAR (Sound of Los Angeles Records), a popular 1970s record label formed by attorney Griffey along with Don Cornelius, the host of the celebrated television dance show *Soul Train,* which Griffey helped start. SOLAR's main act was Shalimar and the Whispers, who helped the label achieve four top 10 hits in England in just one year, as well as success stateside. The label's fame somewhat subsided as the black industry shifted from disco to dance to hip-hop, and Griffey was eager to have a stake in the new style, offering Knight studio and office space for his new label.

Eager to leave Ruthless, Dre told Knight he would happily work with him in a new venture, though he first needed to handle his contract with Eazy's label as well as obligations to record an additional album with Ruthless group Above the Law, as specified by the label's distribution deal with Sony Records. According to a 1989 deal, Dre was to produce a number of albums that Sony would distribute. SOLAR had a similar deal with Sony, and once Dre was in-house, Griffey told Sony representatives they should contact him should they want Dre to produce any albums. They instantly replied, asking if Dre could produce the soundtrack to the up-coming urban drama *Deep Cover.* Working on behalf of Dre, Griffey asked Sony for $1 million because Ruthless had cut off all of Dre's income. The money would also be spent getting Dre released from Ruthless, Griffey told Sony, making Dre's work on *Deep Cover* legal. Sony agreed, and Dre immediately invited Eazy to the SOLAR studios. Eazy arrived unarmed and alone and later claimed that Knight and Dre used strong-arm tactics to secure Dre's release.

"It was like The Godfather," Ruthless attorney Michael Borbeau later told reporter Ronin Ro. "Sony wanted Dre, who was a very hot producer, so they had releases drafted for Knight to bring to Eric Wright (Eazy-E). They wanted him to sign the papers. And if he didn't sign the papers, he knew the consequences" (Ro, 1999, p. 54).

Released from Ruthless, Dre was free to pursue a label with Knight, which they initially called Futureshock in honor of a George Clinton song. Almost immediately, Eazy sued Sony for breach of contract, claiming Dre still needed to produce an album for Ruthless act Above the Law. Sources report that Sony retaliated by claiming that Ruthless came up short on several of their releases, which were commercial failures, something Sony claimed was Eazy's fault because he began using producers other than Dre. Because of this, Sony maintained that Ruthless was responsible for breach of contract but would let them off with a deal: let Above the Law record a song with Dre that could be use on the *Deep Cover* soundtrack, and all would be well. According to writer Ronin Ro, Eazy agreed, though he and Heller continued to warn Sony against working with Knight and filed RICO, or racketeering, charges against both Futureshock and Sony. Soon Eazy's efforts paid off, and Sony cut off all funding to the young label (Ro, 1998, pp. 59–61, 82)

Without any money to record albums, Knight sound solid funding for his and Dre's new venture. And even though Dre and Eazy weren't friendly, the Ruthless rapper did help set Death Row in motion. "A young man by the name of Eric had told me about Suge's background, and that Suge was aware of my background, and that he was somewhat intrigued behind my past and he had wanted to hook up with me in some form or fashion," said Michael "Harry-O" Harris, a former drug kingpin who claims to have initially funded Death Row Records. Harris made these statements in the 2001 documentary *Welcome to Death Row* from the jail that has been his home for more than two decades. "I made the hook-up and we talked on the phone a few times."

Through lawyer David Kenner, Knight was able to visit Harris in jail, where the two discussed funding the new label. Knight told Harris it would cost approximately $1.5 million to start the new venture, with Harris having a 50 percent stake in the company and Dre and Knight each holding 25 percent. Harris authorized his wife, Lydia Harris, and Kenner to transfer the money, forming a company called Godfather Entertainment. Harris's name would not be associated with the company, which would be under only Knight and Kenner's names. The two men didn't tell Harris, though, that they had also formed a second company called Death Row Records, which was not associated with the Godfather name. The money meant for Godfather was instead deposited into Death Row and used to carpet and stock the studio with new speakers and some other new pieces of equipment (Ro, 1999, pp. 76–80).

Within a short time, Dre began work on what would become one of the most influential albums in rap history, though the group still did not have enough money to fund the label, nor did they have a distribution deal to even release albums. In 1992 they got what they needed from Interscope, a newly formed independent label financed and distributed through Time Warner. The small company gave $10 million to Death Row, and within months, Dre's *The Chronic* was released; soon after that, Snoop Doggy

Dogg's *Doggystyle* debuted on the charts at no. 1. Together, the two albums grossed more than $60 million within a year, making Death Row a rather profitable investment. Death Row definitely had power in the industry, something Knight well knew.

A BAD BOY IS BORN

Responsible for several of Uptown's biggest hits, Combs also began to feel his power in the industry, and the man who was once a shy, polite intern was now a loud, opinionated, arrogant man who often said his name on Uptown artist remixes. He soon clashed with the label's new general manager, a white man who questioned Combs's expenses and attitude. Combs grew even louder in his dissent against management, and he continued to promote Bad Boy and his controversial signings, most notably Wallace.

MCA now heavily funded Uptown, gaining access to its catalog. Soon they halted the release of Wallace's song "Dreams (of Fuckin' an R&B Bitch)," an exercise in imagination of all the women Wallace would like to have sex with, including several on the MCA label. The record suffered the chance of never seeing the light of day because MCA and Uptown held the masters and weren't interested in releasing the song.

Uptown also wasn't interested in working with Combs anymore, and he was fired in July 2003. He was tearfully escorted from the Uptown buildings the day Harrell delivered the news. At the time, Harrell reportedly said, "There can only be one lion in the jungle...You're ready...go make it happen" (Coker, 2003, p. 85).

Chapter 3

BECOMING A BAD BOY

Upon leaving Uptown, Combs took with him the Notorious B.I.G. as well as Craig Mack, an artist Combs met while Mack was on tour with EPMD, working as a roadie. Through Uptown, Mack had appeared on a remix of Mary J. Blige's "You Don't Have to Worry," which had brought him some popularity. Wallace was still riding the crest of his successful solo single, "Party and Bullshit," though he was eager to work more on his full-length album, one in which he'd already invested much time and effort. Although he didn't write his lyrics down on paper, Wallace knew what he wanted to say and was ready to step into the studio.

But even with the two artists, Combs wasn't sure he'd make it, often questioning what he was doing, but all the while needing to reassure Wallace and Mack that their albums would get made and that their decision to go with Combs to Bad Boy would be a good one.

"I was scared to death," Combs later told a reporter. "I knew I wanted to get to the point of Berry Gordy and Quincy Jones, but I wasn't thinking of how they got to that point. I was forced to handle a situation, and then I had to grow up real quick."

By then Combs was just 23, a young age for a man to start his own label. But he was lucky in that the seeds for Bad Boy were already sown: he had pushed the name of the label while still with Uptown, mentioning it to some of the industry heavies he had met through Harrell, and he had artists like Wallace give shout-outs on remixes, both marketing ploys that he hoped would have solid returns.

Bringing in old friends Harve Pierre, Mark Pitts, and Nashiem Myrick, he set up shop in an extra bedroom of his mother's Mount Vernon house, with work days that began early—usually about 8 A.M.—his mother's living room piled with papers while friends worked, usually taking turns on Combs's only computer. Combs—along with lawyer Kenny Meiselas—worked day and night to find funding for Bad Boy.

A friend offered space at his Scarsdale house, and Myrick built a small home studio that, thought not state of the art, was fully capable of getting the job done. In that studio, Wallace, Mack, and a female group called Total recorded, while Combs and Kenny Meiselas hustled to find funding.

And although they didn't have much, they did have a vision and some raw backing talent, especially in Wallace. All they needed was someone who understood setbacks and could easily get on board with the company Combs wanted to create, one where he ran the show, producing albums that would receive acclaim as well as sell. Combs needed someone who believed in him the way he believed in himself, regardless of any recent setbacks.

And soon Combs found that person, someone who had also suffered several stumbles, but who had the vision and the initiative to get back up, dust himself off, and still become a force in the music industry.

ENTER ARISTA

Born in an impoverished area of Brooklyn in 1932, Clive Davis was always one to face the odds, having earned a full scholarship to Harvard Law School after graduating at the top of his class at a public college. Once he became a lawyer, he took a job at a small firm with several big clients, including CBS Records. His work impressed his clients, and he was soon hired full-time at the label, which then was a subsidiary of Columbia Records.

Once at CBS, he met label head Goodard Lieberson, who instantly liked the charismatic Davis. Lieberson took Davis under his wing, and Davis worked his way up from one of several staff lawyers to become president of CBS Records in 1967. Once in his new position, Davis fully embraced the world of rock, as well as folk, seeing potential in the changing music landscape that so many other executives ignored. After signing folk artist Donovan, Davis began to seek other avenues and, on a whim, decided to attend the pivotal Monterey Pop Festival, a three-day event held in Monterey, California, that brought more than 200,000 people to watch dozens of performers, all of whom performed for free. Jimi Hendrix made his American debut at the festival, and Janis Joplin performed before a huge crowd for the very first time. There Davis witnessed a world he'd only seen on television, and he immediately knew this was the direction he wanted to take CBS. He immediately offered contracts for Janis Joplin and Jimi Hendrix, as well as several others. Within a few years, and after attending other such events, Davis signed other pivotal artists, including Bruce Springsteen, Billy Joel, Pink Floyd and Earth, Wind and Fire.

But, as with Combs and many others, his successes came with controversy, and in 1972 Davis was fired from CBS amid accusations he used company money for personal expenses. He was immediately hired at Columbia Pictures, where he worked as a consultant for their various music projects while penning his memoirs. In 1976, Davis was convicted of tax evasion but was fined only $10,000, an amount he easily paid. The next year, Davis became president of Columbia's record division, and he immediately merged three separate labels at Columbia, forming Arista, which he bought most of from Columbia. Arista quickly became a top label with high-selling acts, including Toni Braxton, Aretha Franklin, and Whitney Houston. But Davis, recognizing the power of rap as it continued to grab national attention, wanted to get in on the action and sought out opportunities to fund a small label. He had heard Naughty by Nature's "OPP," had been impressed by several other rap albums, and wanted to become more involved with the genre he felt would soon take hold of the music industry.

Through a mutual friend, Combs was introduced to Davis, and the two instantly hit it off, finding in each other qualities the other admired: being able to stand tall after having fallen hard, an ear for innovative music, and the ability to make things happen, often making something out of nothing, or, in the case of Bad Boy, next to nothing.

Davis gave Combs $1.5 million, a small amount in an industry where even studio time can costs thousands an hour. Combs used part of the money to buy back from Uptown the songs Wallace and Mack had already recorded, as well as to negotiate the release of Smalls, Faith Evans, Total, and Craig Mack. He reinvested the remaining funds in Bad Boy, building its marketing efforts while giving additional money to recording, knowing that if the label released strong, solid albums with a formidable street presence, the rest would fall into place.

And it did. Combs was soon able to negotiate even more money for distribution and for recording, knowing that now his future lay in that overweight rapper with a lazy eye, the man now called Notorious.

Not long after Wallace's demo made it into *The Source*'s "Unsigned Hype" column, Wallace had befriended its author, Matty C, who lived just a few blocks away. Through his connections with *The Source*, Matty C often received new copies of albums before they hit the streets, including a small gem from a West Coast producer Wallace had always admired for his work with N.W.A. Once he hit play on the tape deck, though, Wallace knew he was listening to something like nothing he'd ever heard before, an album that crossed all barriers and inspired him to lyrically go places he had never explored before.

THE CHRONIC

Easily one of the most innovative records in music history, Dr. Dre's *The Chronic* transformed not only the way rap was perceived but also the way it was received, most notably by mainstream audiences. Released in late 1992, *The Chronic* is considered one of the most important albums in rap history, paving the way for rap to not only enter mainstream markets to do so in a way that didn't force Dr. Dre or any of the artists on the album to succumb to any sort of industry pressure to be more "white" or to have more of a pop sound. Its three main singles—"Nuthin' But a G Thang," "Dre Day," and "Let Me Ride"—all hit top spots on the Billboard charts, and its videos played in constant rotation on MTV and BET.

Featuring a battery of rappers, including the recently discovered Snoop Doggy Dogg, Dre was able to step into a world previously unknown to a rapper, even the superstar sort Dre had already become. Once kept confined to "urban" stations and in video blocks such as Yo MTV! Raps, Mary J. Blige's "Real Love" was sometimes played alongside Nirvana's "Smells Like Teen Spirit," and the pop group Spin Doctors gave way to Dr. Dre, who was now as much music icon as rock star, his image blazoned on key chains and t-shirts sold at kiosks in malls and his poster on the walls of thousands of record shops and his marijuana leaf–blazoned baseball caps the culprit in many a kid's suspension from school.

Why this album, filled with countless incendiary references to Eazy-E and Jerry Heller, was the one to bring rap to the forefront still is unclear, though it was rather innovative, incorporating tough, gangsta lyrics with smooth, attractive beats and samples that made even the stodgiest person nod his head. The album also moves seamlessly from one song to the next, and the lazy California style of delivery made the album unrestricted to many who weren't able to jump into the harder, faster East Coast rap available to a mainstream audience.

And for these reasons, *The Chronic* found international success; it was widely accessible for all sorts of audiences ranging from the suburban white teen to a hustler on the streets of Brooklyn, such as Christopher Wallace. Although Wallace did use *The Chronic* as inspiration, he was already determined to make an album that could speak to anyone anywhere before hearing *The Chronic*. "It ain't Brooklyn shit," he once told a reporter. "It's the shit that niggas in Houston can get with. Shit that niggas in

Idaho can get with. It's just reality laid out on the table" (Coker, 2003, p. 89). Wallace felt that his album expressed the world he knew and that he lived well the idea that rap had become a black man's CNN, and his depictions of a life of crime and of life spent hustling were as poignant as they were clever.

He at first wanted to name his album *The Teflon Don* in honor of John Gotti, American mobster and head of the Gambino crime family, one of the most famous mob families in history, but Combs suggested *Ready to Die*, which, in the mindset Wallace had while recording the album, seemed more fitting. At that point of his life, Wallace was indeed ready to die because he was still unable to provide for his daughter, his mother was still recovering from her breast surgery, and the only skills he had were those on the street, skills that would end with his being either arrested or killed, or even both, as he'd already seen so many times in the cases of friends and others on the street. He knew that although life held promise, today it was just another day, another struggle, even with Combs's promises that the work would soon pay off and that he would be able to live life as a rapper, not a hustler.

Combs—and Bad Boy—found moderate success with the label's first release. Within several months of Bad Boy's official inception, Mack's single "Flava In Ya Ear" was the first to bear the Bad Boy imprint. The song was successful in a crossover market, peaking at no. 9 on the Billboard Hot 100 charts. The song's remix spotlighted Wallace, but also included Busta Rhymes, LL Cool J., and rapper Rampage. Wildly popular in New York, the song furthered established the buzz surrounding Wallace, who also appeared in the equally popular video.

Project: Funk Da World, Mack's debut album, released a few months later, was moderately popular, reaching only gold status more than a year later. Produced by Easy Mo Bee, the album's three singles—"Flava In Ya Ear," "Making Moves with Puff," and "Get Down"—also enjoyed some popularity, though not as much as the remixed "Flava In Ya Ear" released before the album hit the streets. His song "Get Down" was the album's only real crossover hit, peaking just at no. 38 on the Billboard Hot 100 chart. The album featured only one guest—Combs, on the song "Making Moves with Puff," a move many later criticized. The timing of the album was also criticized because it came out just six days after the pivotal *Ready to Die*.

READY TO DIE

Released September 13, 1994, *Ready to Die* brought attention back to the East Coast. Recorded at the Hit Factory between 1993 and 1994, the album is a mix of dark songs along with some lighter songs, largely because of the time between the album's two recording sessions, which spanned decidedly different parts of Wallace's life. The more somber, darker lyrics were penned largely when Wallace was first signed to Uptown, when Jan Jackson was carrying his child, his mother had breast cancer, and he was still hustling to bring in money. In these sessions, Wallace's performance has been described as "inexperienced, higher-pitched," with Wallace's delivery as "hungry and paranoid" ("The Making of *Ready to Die*," 2006). His later sessions, recorded after Combs left Uptown and formed Bad Boy Records, have been described as having a "a smoother, more confident vocal tone," lending to more radio-ready tracks with a lighter tone. At this time, Wallace no longer wrote in notebooks, instead keeping all his music inside his head, freestyling when it came time to deliver. He was one of the first known rappers to use this method, though other artists, such as Nas and Jay-Z, later copied it. Wallace also recorded most of the album while stoned or drunk, a standard for many artists, though his method often came at a high price because he would often spend hours in the studio preparing to rhyme before he actually got anything down on tape. At high-priced studios like the Hit Factory, where much of the album was recorded, recording costs could quickly mount. Wallace also often brought women into the studio, and there are countless anecdotes of Wallace's sexual life, including one situation between Wallace and two women in a back room, an encounter from which Wallace immediately went back to work, nodding to DJ Premier to start rolling. Wallace closed his eyes, and soon the lyrics for "Unbelievable" rolled off his tongue, three perfect sets of lyrics he was able to record in less than an hour. That itself was unbelievable.

But that's how Wallace recorded, waiting until the moment he felt it to have the record button pushed and his voice captured. Some producers grew weary of this process, though those who often worked with Wallace, like Easy Mo Bee and DJ Premier, knew his style and knew he would always deliver.

And deliver he did. *Ready to Die* starts with an introduction that seemingly tells the story of Wallace's life, beginning with his birth and then moving to his childhood and onto his music, in a section that samples Snoop Doggy Dogg's "The Shiznit," offering homage to the prominence of West Coast rap. Throughout the album, heavy, somber songs ("Everyday Struggle," "The What") are balanced with lighter, sexier romps ("Big Poppa," "Unbelievable"). The album ends with "Suicidal Thoughts," a chilling song that ultimately has Wallace contemplating suicide while on the phone with Combs, telling the producer all the reasons why he shouldn't live. Through the song, Combs grows increasingly frantic until, finally, the listener hears gunshots and then an operator's voice saying the phone is off the hook as a heartbeat slows to a stop.

Almost every track represented a facet of Wallace's life, such as with "Things Done Changed," which was meant to represent Brooklyn, how Wallace and his friends grew up, and the life they led on the streets. The album is largely autobiographical and contains many references to Wallace's real world, including his mother's diagnosis of breast cancer ("Things Done Changed"), his early dreams of becoming a rap star ("Juicy"), and, maybe most of all, his time spent hustling ("Everyday Struggle," "Things Done Changed," "Warning," "Gimme the Loot," and "The What"). Wallace wrote all the songs himself, and Easy Mo Bee and Chucky Thompson were the main producers, though Combs is listed on many of the songs as a producer. The album features samples of many other songs, including ones by the Isley Brothers, Kool and the Gang, Miles Davis, Gang Starr, Isaac Hayes, the Honeydrippers, Dr. Dre, and the Sugarhill Gang.

The album's three singles—"Juicy," "Big Poppa," and "One More Chance"—all fared well on the charts, peaking at no. 27, no. 6, and no. 2, respectively, on the Billboard Hot 100. Both "Big Poppa" and "One More Chance" were no. 1 on the Billboard Hot Rap Tracks, and "Juicy" peaked at no. 3. The singles, along with their videos, were the album's only real radio-friendly songs. All were commercial successes, with "Juicy" eventually reaching gold status and the other two reaching platinum status. "One More Chance" was the most successful song on the album, though its remix, featuring both Faith Evans and Mary J. Blige, was surprisingly not as successful.

The album was released to great reviews, having achieved the coveted five mics in *The Source*. It is the third highest ranked rap album of all time, coming in just below Public Enemy's *It Takes a Nation of Millionsto Hold Us Back* and Run D.M.C.'s *Raising Hell*. Many publications have listed the album in its list of top releases, including *XXL*, *Vibe*, *Rolling Stone*, *Spin*, and *The Source*.

Released in the same year as the Wu Tang Clan's highly influential *Enter the Wu-Tang Clan (36 Chambers)* as well as Nas's critically-acclaimed *Illmatic*, Wallace's *Ready to Die* helped wrestle back the spotlight from the gangsta rap of the West Coast, taking prominence on the charts that Dr. Dre and Snoop Doggy Dogg had held for two years.

RAP'S RECLAMATION OF NEW YORK

Born of the infamous Bronx block parties in the late 1970s, hip-hop came from a competition between locals and West Indian DJs, who separated the percussion in funk and disco songs from the other musical elements, using a turntable to rearrange the percussion into entirely different songs altogether. Soon two turntables and a mixer were used to combine elements from various songs, creating a whole new composition, and eventually New York DJs such as Grandmaster Flash and Afrika Bambataa used these new songs as background for what was quickly known as rapping. In the beginning, rap was usually little more than introductions and homage to the rapper himself or to other musicians, though eventually the lyrics expanded to incorporate other material.

This history rooted in New York has always lent to the city being considered not just the genre's birthplace but also its capital; for many years, almost all innovations in the style came from New York, including scratching and beatboxing. The strongest examples of hip-hop innovation also hailed from the streets of the Big Apple, seen most especially in Erik B. and Rakim's *Paid in Full*, a visionary album that showcased not only Rakim's expansive lyrical ability but also Eric B.'s extensive use of soul and R&B albums, which would prove fundamental in hip-hop's development. *Paid in Full* moved rap from the old-school style of the Sugar hill Gang and Run D.M.C.—known for simpler, more basic beats and raps—to the new-school style, which showcased faster lyrical delivery heavily nuanced by clever metaphors.

Even though the East Coast held tight the history of rap, rap's future seemed to rest with the West, as was proved by the phenomenal success of N.W.A. and their release *Straight Outta Compton*, an album that redefined rap as well as helped bring the style to the forefront of mainstream music. There was also another West Coast rapper changing the landscape of rap, one whose socially charged lyrics took away from the gangsta-rap style of N.W.A.

TUPAC SHAKUR

Born Lesane Parish Crooks, Tupac Shakur was raised among controversy that would follow him forever. His mother, Afeni, whose real name was Alice Faye Williams, claimed to be a member of the Black Panthers and was pregnant with Shakur when she was arrested on 156 counts of conspiracy against the government and New York landmarks. She was later acquitted, but carried Shakur while briefly imprisoned awaiting trial, often fighting for food and living in what were later described as substandard conditions. Shortly after her release, she delivered Shakur.

Shakur never knew his father, although his mother offered two possible candidates: a man named Billy Garland and a hustler named Legs, both of whom she was sleeping with around the time Shakur was conceived. She was married to Mutulu Shakur at the time, but she always maintained he could not have fathered her baby. While Shakur was still a toddler, his godfather, Elmer "Geronimo" Pratt, was convicted of murdering a schoolteacher during a 1968 robbery, and Shakur's stepfather, Mutulu, was wanted in part for having helped his sister, Assata Shakur, Shakur's godmother, to escape from prison in New Jersey, where she had been incarcerated for shooting two state troopers to death in 1973.

Years later, Mutulu was found guilty of armed robbery of a Brinks armored car, a heist that ended with two police officers and a guard dead. Having run from the law for four years, Mutulu Shakur was placed on the FBI's Ten Most Wanted fugitive list before finally being captured in 1986. Sentenced to 60 years, Mutulu left behind any chance of reconciling with his family, including his stepson Tupac, who had spent most his young life without any sort of male role model.

Shakur's mother divorced Mutulu when the future rapper was a small child, though he remained a presence in Shakur's life throughout his early years. His mother took a job as a paralegal to support her small family, which included a younger daughter, Shakur's half-sister Sekyiwa Shakur, and his older stepbrother, Mopreme "Komani" Shakur, who would later appear on several of Shakur's recordings. The young Tupac was a child actor, most notably playing Travis in a production of *A Raisin in the Sun* at the famed 127th Street Ensemble in Harlem, with Shakur being the acting troupe's most famous member. But Afeni started seeing Legs again, and the couple dabbled in drugs, particularly crack. After Legs was arrested for credit card fraud, Afeni decided it was time to leave New York behind, having set her sights on Baltimore, Maryland. There Shakur played up his big city roots by rapping under the name MC New York. His friend Dana "Mouse" Smith often accompanied Shakur as a beatbox, and the two won several school talent shows and local rap competitions and became rather popular.

Shakur then went to the Baltimore School for Arts, where he met Jada Pinkett, an actress who would become one of his best friends, in a friendship that lasted throughout his short life. Shakur once said of Pinkett, "Jada is my heart. She will be my friend for my whole life." In the same documentary, *Tupac Resurrection*, Pinkett named Shakur as "one of my best friends. He was like a brother. It was beyond friendship for us. The type of relationship we had, you only get that once in a lifetime."

In Baltimore, the Shakur family lived in an impoverished neighborhood overrun with violence and gangs. After a young boy Shakur's age was shot and killed steps away from their front door, Afeni decided to send her children to live with family in Marin City, a small, rather poor town 10 miles outside of San Francisco. Conditions there weren't much better than in Baltimore, although the children were saved from the downfall their mother soon took, when she began smoking crack again and all but cut off contact with her Shakur, his brother, and his sister.

It was in Marin City that Shakur met a white, single mother named Leila Steinberg. She quickly invited him to live at her house, and she became his manager as he attended Tamalpais High School. He also joined the Ensemble Theater Company, eager to pursue his career in entertainment. Steinberg had several connections, having known Atron Gregory, the executive who ran TNT Records and managed Digital Underground, for a few years. She was able to secure Shakur a spot as a backup dancer on Digital Underground tour, with his biggest role being to air hump during their hit "Humpty Dance." When the band went back into the studio, they invited Shakur, who delivered a few lines to the single "Same Song" on their 1991 album *This Is an EP Release*. He toured with the band on that album.

Invigorated about rap, Shakur soon recorded a demo, using his connections with TNT to have it delivered to Tommy Boy executive Monica Lynch. She saw Shakur's promise but passed on his demo, passing it along to Tom Whalley, an A&R rep with the burgeoning Interscope Records. He instantly loved the album and handed it off to Interscope head Ted Field, who used his teenage daughter as a gauge to see how well it might be received by the younger white kids who were increasingly becoming rap's audience. She loved it, and Interscope instantly signed Shakur. Within just a few months, he recorded *2Pacalypse Now*, which sold 500,000 copies, leading Time Warner to increases its stake in Interscope. Many hailed the album as a realistic and gritty view of life on the streets, free from the glorification found on many other rap albums. *2Pacalypse Now* featured the hit "Brenda's Got a Baby," which tells the story of 12-year-old Brenda, a dim, impoverished girl who becomes pregnant with her cousin's child. Without any options, or a family that cares, she first sells crack—and then her body—to feed herself and her child. The song received national attention for spotlighting the growing problem of teen pregnancy and the almost nonexistent support from the baby's father, the teen's family, and the government.

Songs like "Brenda's Got a Baby" pushed Shakur into the role of spokesperson for the plight of the poor living in a ghetto, a role he eagerly undertook in his usual poetic fashion. But even with his increasingly positive career, the controversy that had always followed Shakur soon reared its head: Shakur was in a gunfight that struck and killed six-year-old Qa'id

Walker-Teal. Shakur did not pull the trigger on the gun that killed the child and was never charged in connection with the murder, yet he still carried responsibility for Qa'id's death, later settling with the family in a wrongful death suit.

With his recording career on solid ground, Shakur also took to the screen, making his first film appearance in the 1991 comedy *Nothing But Trouble*, which starred Dan Aykroyd, Demi Moore, Chevy Chase, and John Candy, as well as members of Digital Underground, who all held minor roles, as did Shakur. His first starring role was in the 1992 drama *Juice* as Bishop, a trigger-happy teen who accidentally kills a friend before setting out on a small murder spree to cover his tracks. A year later, Shakur starred opposite Janet Jackson in *Poetic Justice*, a dramatic romance in which Jackson and Shakur had several romantic scenes. Jackson required proof of a negative HIV test before agreeing to any of those scenes (Weiner, 2004). Shakur also played Birdie in *Above the Rim*, using his connections to Wallace and other real-life hustlers to research the role and using the style of method actor, a style he would later repeat in his rap career as he began living out the roles he'd created in his songs. This was when he and Wallace became close, with Wallace still a relatively unknown rapper. Shakur, handsome and well spoken with a few movies and a successful debut album, seemed the sort of person Wallace wanted to know.

Although Tupac Shakur and Christopher Wallace had a bit in common, their friendship was also heavily based on what the other had, be it street credit or skills. For Wallace, Shakur had grown up living the life Wallace could only rap about; Shakur was raised amid abject poverty with a mother who not only was jailed when she was pregnant with Shakur, but also had a rotating cast of men as a possible father and a persistent drug addiction that often left the family in shambles, as she withered away to a crackhead. On the other hand, Wallace had a skill Shakur admired, as well as a raw quality he didn't feel he had—Wallace was a natural on the microphone and never practiced his lyrics or his style, both of which were widely acclaimed.

Shakur lived in Los Angeles at the time, and the two friends visited each other often, sleeping on each other's couches. The two also recorded a few duets, including "Runnin'" as well as "Let's Get It On," both of which were released in 1994. They recorded a third song as well, which included friend Randy "Stretch" Walker and was meant for use on *Ready to Die*, but Combs eventually scrapped the song, claiming it didn't fit with the rest of the album.

Wallace and Shakur also occasionally performed together, including the now-famous show at the Budweiser Superfest in October 1993 at Madison Square Garden, where many noteworthy performers have played, including Big Daddy Kane, who introduced Shakur to Easy Mo Bee. But despite their close friendship, things quickly fell apart, resulting in a massive East–West rivalry, a war that many felt started at a New York studio in late 1994.

That was the same year Shakur released *Strictly 4 My N.I.G.G.A.Z.*, a strong follow-up to his debut, *2Pacalypse Now*. The album featured the same social and political themes that first attracted fans to Shakur, and it debuted at no. 24 on the Billboard 200 and had two no. 1 hits: "Keep Ya Head Up" and "I Get Around." Soon after the album's release, Shakur formed the group Thug Life with several friends, including rappers Big Syke, Macadoshis, Rated R, and Tupac's stepbrother Mopreme Shakur. Christopher Wallace was originally set to be a member of the group, but Combs wouldn't allow it, wanting Wallace to instead focus on his own career. Both Wallace and Shakur understood, though they still often sought opportunities to work together.

Shakur soon moved to Atlanta to focus more on his career; "the dirty South" was beginning to come into its own, boasting a formidable scene largely centered around the Dungeon Family, the group associated with Outkast and Killer Mike, as well as So So Def, Jermaine Dupri's landmark record label. Also from Atlanta was the increasingly popular Ludacris and the infamous Freaknik spring break celebration, which is where Shakur was first introduced to Wallace through his single "Party and Bullshit," a song he liked as soon as he heard it.

But as with many things in Shakur's life, things in Atlanta soon fell apart. In late October 1993, Shakur was arrested after shooting two off-duty officers he felt were harassing a black motorist. The officers, two brothers, were later revealed to be drunk at the time, having stolen weapons from the Atlanta Police Department evidence room. Neither officer was on duty at the time Shakur shot them, though they were in their cruiser and pulled someone over as officers. The charges against Shakur were eventually dropped, though he was never reimbursed for the money he spent on lawyers.

And his lawyer fees were quickly mounting. He was charged with assault in 1993 and, later in the year, with a sexual offense that led to his imprisonment. In December 1993, Shakur was charged with sodomy and sexual abuse of Ayanna Jackson, a 19-year-old woman who had come to his New York hotel room a few days after having oral sex with the rapper on the dance floor of a popular club and later returning with him to his hotel room, where the two had consensual sex. She claimed that she returned to his room a few days later, at which point she again had some sort of sexual contact with Shakur as well as his friends, whom she says gang raped her. Shakur always claimed he was asleep at the time of the alleged assault, waking only when she accused of him of encouraging the attack, asking "How could you do this to me?" Though he later admitted guilt at leaving her alone in the room with his friends, he always maintained that he did not abuse her and that he did not encourage others to do so. He was later convicted of "sexual abuse (forcibly touching the buttocks)" in what the presiding judge would describe as an "act of brutal violence against a helpless woman" (James, 1995).

In interviews, Shakur said he knew that the men—promoter Jaques Agnant and road manager Charles "Man" Fuller—planned to have sex with her. Shakur admitted that he did nothing to stop them, citing an unspoken rap code that allowed anyone to sleep with groupies, leaving only someone's "girl" off-limits. For Shakur to speak up and stop the men would mean he claimed her as his, he later said. He left the room, leaving her to the two large men, a decision Shakur later said he would regret forever. But before his trial, while hanging out with Damien "D-Roc" Butler and Wallace in his hotel room, Shakur clowned about the event, pulling out a small wireless microphone he'd recently purchased.

"From now on, bitch wanna...[mess] with me, I'm getting it all on tape," he told Wallace, both laughing (Coker, 2003, p. 127). The exchange was caught on tape by filmmaker Dream Hampton, as were other moments of the happy night when the old friends let down their guards and let go of the world and simply relaxed.

But that would be one of the last such nights for the old friends. Just a few months later, Shakur's trial began. On November 24, 1994, while standing on the sidewalk outside the courtroom, a wild-eyed Shakur told a local broadcast station, "It's not a crime for me to be with anybody I want to be with. But it is a crime for that girl to turn it into a rape charge....It was her who, at the dance floor, who [sic] had oral sex with me. She should be charged, not me."

But that single event—and the domino effect that followed—easily changed Shakur's life forever and, in most ways, for the worst. He went bankrupt fighting the charges, and the negative press led to fewer producers and directors wanting to work with the actor, who was convicted of assault after attacking Menace II Society director Allen Hughes after an argument over the role Hughes offered to Shakur in the movie, one the actor felt would depict him in a negative light. He was later sentenced to 15 days in jail for the attack. But as things slowly unraveled for Shakur, things were finally coming together for Wallace as his hit Ready to Die continued to climb the charts.

Chapter 4

LIVING THE LARGE LIFE

Almost as soon as *Ready to Die* hit the streets, Wallace became a well-respected rapper, gathering positive reviews and accolades from coast to coast. Despite being rather overweight with a lazy eye, Wallace was considered somewhat of a sex symbol with solid street credit. His rap style, charming while at the same time realistic to the struggles of a small-time hustler, found a wide audience among many rap fans, a path well paved by the earlier success of *The Chronic*.

As critically hailed as other acclaimed East Coast albums—mainly Nas's *Illmatic* and Wu Tang Clan's *Enter the Wu-Tang (36 Chambers)*—*Ready to Die* also found massive commercial success, bringing with it increased attention back to New York. Reviews were overwhelmingly positive, with one critic claiming that Wallace had a talent for "painting a sonic picture so vibrant that you're transported right to the scene," and with another claiming he used "the natural rapping, clever use of sound effects and acted dialogue, and concept element...[to] set this well apart from the average gangsta bragging" ("Review: *Ready to Die*," 1994).

In his neighborhoods, songs off his album roared from boom boxes and car stereo systems, and, like when he was a hustler, Wallace was a center of gravity in his neighborhood. In the beginning, Wallace met reporters at his apartment or on the streets of Bedford-Stuyvesant, including ones from the formidable *New York Times* and *The Source*. In one such interview, Wallace took *Vibe* reporter Cheo Hodari Coker with him as he walked through the neighborhood, stopping often to talk to friends and hustlers. During their walk, Coker witnessed a scene where Wallace acted as if he couldn't find his gun to loan to some kids wanting to hit someone up for their VCR. Wallace said, of the disparity in the neighborhood, in a negative view of the inner city, "You're going to do something, man, you can't just sit there because that's what really hurts parents the most, to just watch their son give up and not do nothing to fix it" (Coker, 2003, p. 106).

But that is what brought Wallace to where he was that day. At that point, he stayed put because he felt it was the best thing for him to do. To move to a nicer home in a nicer neighborhood would make him less real to his fans, and he somehow would lack as their spokesperson.

But to remain in his violent, impoverished neighborhood made him a target, something Wallace knew intimately, having run those streets himself. He began to keep the house in a tight lockdown, stockpiling guns and keeping them under his mattress and beneath his pillow, ready to protect his small family if anything were to happen.

And soon, after a Bad Boy promotional shoot, that family expanded. In late July 1994, Wallace met through a mutual friend the singer Faith Evans, a light-skinned woman whose beauty and attitude instantly captivated the young rapper. Half black and half Italian, Evans was raised without a father; he left the family when Evans was a young girl. From early childhood, Evans sang in her church choir and is rumored to have often brought tears to the eyes of those who heard her voice, a soprano that has been described as rain. Always studious, Evans did well in high school and was accepted to New York's Fordham University, which she attended for less than a year before dropping out to actively pursue music. She began dating Kiyamma Griffin, a producer who worked with Combs. Soon she was pregnant, and she often accompanied Griffin to his studio sessions, including one with Usher. According to legend, a back-up vocalist dropped out at the last minute, and Griffin allegedly spoke up—"My girlfriend is a singer"—and Combs waved her over to a microphone. She took in hand the music, and after she had sung a few notes, Combs wanted to sign her to Uptown as a backup singer. Soon on the label's roster, Evans often performed background vocals for other acts, including Mary J. Blige, and wrote several songs for both Blige and the popular Color Me Badd.

When Combs left Uptown to form Bad Boy, Evans soon followed, largely because Combs promised she would soon have her own album, something she had dreamed of for years. Once formally signed to the label, Evans was embraced by the Bad Boy family, and it was at a Bad Boy promotional shoot that she met Wallace, who was shy and quiet around the beautiful Evans. She was nervous, talking rapidly to fill the void in the air, though she later said he had a charm about him that instantly attracted her. Wallace asked for a ride home to Brooklyn, and she happily agreed. She later said they simply chatted on the way home, pregnant pauses often filling the air as one would smile at the other, sometimes laughing. The two ended up spending the afternoon alone together in his room, and Evans later said she felt sure she wouldn't talk to him again anytime soon. But she was wrong. Wallace called Evans within just a few hours, having copied her number off promotional photos from the shoot, and asked her out to see a movie. They went to the Newport Center Mall in Jersey City, where they window-shopped hand in hand, oblivious to the world, including the movie they saw, which Evans can't recall.

The two became inseparable, and less than two weeks later, Wallace asked her to marry him. Though their connection was quick, it was deep, and the two had many things in common. Both had daughters, and both were raised by a single mother without a father actively in the picture. Both were burgeoning players in New York's hip-hop scene, though Evans was more on the R&B side. Both worked hard and often, spending most free time in the studio. And both wanted to be with the other, regardless of how rushed their relationship was. So on August 4, 1994, the two married before a justice of the peace in Rosslyn, New York, a small town upstate. He wore jeans and a button-down shirt; she wore a summer dress and sandals.

The two immediately returned to work after an hours-long honeymoon. After work, Wallace went home to the apartment he still shared with his mother. He told her he had gotten married earlier that day, though she didn't believe him. The next day, though, one of her friends called to tell her Wallace was saying hello to his wife on a popular radio show. Voletta Wallace immediately flipped on the nearest radio, and just like with his music career, it took a radio announcement for Voletta Wallace to believe her son.

Wallace kept the two women apart for weeks, much to his mother's anger. It wasn't until Evans called for Wallace one day that she finally spoke with Voletta, who immediately chastised the young woman. "Don't you have a momma?" she allegedly asked Evans, adding that she should have known better than to have ignored her. After a brief conversation, both Voletta Wallace and Evans realized that Christopher had kept the two apart for no real reason past his anticipation that his mother would dislike Evans. But to his surprise, the two instantly became friends and occasionally even spent time together, even after the young married couple had moved into a large loft apartment in Brooklyn's Fort Greene neighborhood.

Within weeks of moving into the their new home, Wallace left on a promotional tour with Craig Mack, and Evans returned to the studio, working on her debut album, a setup that set the tone for the marriage.

Both were always busy with work, and Wallace, never a one-woman kind of guy, often took advantage of the perks of being a successful musician.

With constant promotion, such as the radio tour with Mack, as well as relentless radio interviews and live performances, *Ready to Die* enjoyed solid sales, and Wallace soon hit the road along with Junior M.A.F.I.A., sleeping in the small tour bus and living off fast food, most often McDonald's. Although some shows sold out, others had only moderate attendance, but one thing became standard: the women. No matter where they were, all the ladies wanted "Big Poppa." Wallace, despite often being dirty, sweaty, and stinky, was still somehow a sex symbol.

Few industries can turn a crack dealer into a sought-after, well-respected musician, a factor many cite as rap's downfall. In a few short months, Wallace went from selling crack on the corner of Fulton Street and St. James Place to performing sold-out shows at $20,000 an appearance, and with the newfound cash came an increased desire to show his wealth. Gone were the clothes of Christopher Wallace, and in their place was a new look that mimicked that of the old gangsters: hats that matched his tailored suits, expensive bottles of champagne and liquor, and a home in New Jersey, where Wallace soon relocated, feeling that his newfound wealth made him a target in Brooklyn.

But even as he separated himself even farther from the streets that first saw him come up, Wallace became heavily involved in a rivalry as cutthroat as that of any street gang, one that ultimately ended in two still-unsolved murders.

Despite the geographical distance—Wallace in New York, Shakur in California—the two were still friends, seeking each other out whenever they were able. One of the times Wallace and Shakur hung out together as friends was at a party Combs threw for himself on September 11, 1994. At the party, Wallace and Shakur spent time in the club's lounge, laughing and smiling like the old friends they were, having met a couple years earlier through mutual acquaintances. That would be the last time the two would laugh together; they wouldn't see each other again for more than two months, when the rappers came face to face as Shakur lay on the floor as elevator doors opened, his body bloody from the five gunshots that had pierced his leg, his groin, and his head.

QUAD STUDIO SHOOTINGS

Cash poor and needing work, in November 1994, Shakur went to Quad Studios in Times Square, where he was set to appear on rapper Little Shawn's album for $7,000. With him was longtime friend Randy

"Stretch" Walker, a man named Fred, and another man named Zayd, who was dating Shakur's sister. As the four men approached the studio from the street, Lil' Cease called to Shakur from an upstairs window, smiling and waving to the men below. Shakur returned the greeting and entered the studio's large lobby.

Just inside the doors sat a black man wearing army fatigues, someone Shakur noted because the man didn't acknowledge him with a hello or even a nod. Shakur, now a famous rapper, wasn't used to this sort of reception, one he later said he would find odd even if he weren't well-known. He also said the fatigues were similar to the kind many were wearing in Brooklyn; camouflaged clothes had recently come back in style in the borough. But because he was stoned, Shakur let it pass, ignoring the man before noticing a second fellow, also wearing fatigues, sitting at a nearby table. Just as the first man had, this man also regarded Shakur with only a brief glance before casting his eyes down, almost as if he were hiding them. Shakur said he and his friends walked to the elevator, hit the "up" button, and waited for the doors to open.

In less than a minute, Shakur turned to find guns turned on him, twin 9 millimeters. The three men with Shakur instantly dropped to the floor, though the rapper himself stood scared, not moving. The men first checked for his gun and then asked for his jewelry and money before firing, hitting Shakur first in his testicles and then in the back of his head. The men turned and left, and Shakur fell to the floor, unconscious.

Cease and Junior M.A.F.I.A.'s Nino Brown rode the elevator down to meet Shakur, though they weren't prepared for the scene that unfolded once the elevator doors opened. Shakur lay on the lobby floor, his blood having stained his jeans and spilled from his head. The armed assailants told Cease and Nino to get back on the elevator, which they did, heading back upstairs to tell the others about the attack. Back in the lobby, the men left, and Shakur and the others slowly stood, lumbering for the door until finally they were on the streets, the lights of Times Square bright as Shakur screamed for help. No one immediately came, and the wounded men went back into the studios, stepping on the elevator. Once the doors opened upstairs, Shakur saw Combs, Wallace, and Andre Harrell from Uptown, among several others, including Little Shawn, who began crying uncontrollably, despite not really knowing Shakur. He was the only one who reacted, Shakur later said, adding that he didn't know why those men were there at Little Shawn's recording.

"I noticed that nobody would look at me. Andre Harrell wouldn't look at me. I had been going to dinner with him the last few days. He had invited me to the set of *New York Undercover*, telling me he was going to get me a job," Shakur later told a *Vibe* reporter while still in prison. "Puffy was standing back too. I knew Puffy. He knew how much stuff I had done for Biggie before he came out" (Powell, 1995).

But Wallace and Combs always claimed to have helped Shakur from the elevator and into a chair. Harrell later said there was nothing unusual about everyone being at the studio. Wallace was already at Quad working on Junior M.A.F.I.A.'s album, and Combs had stopped by to say hello. Harrell was bankrolling Shawn's session, with some other recording sessions with affiliated artists—SWV, Deborah Cox, and Mobb Deep—going on in nearby rooms.

Police were called, but it took nearly 15 minutes for anyone to appear. When officers did arrive, they were brandishing guns and aiming at Wallace and Chico Delvac, the most ominous-looking two of the bunch. According to several sources, almost everyone in the room carried guns, many of those illegal and unregistered.

"It made me realize that the element of energy being young and black right now in the inner city is so violent that young people just feel the need to have that level just in case," Harrell later said. "If it goes there, they got the potential at least to make them back off, because they're prepared to have the final say. And you know, gun play is the final say" (Coker, 2003, p. 134).

Shakur, though, was granted a reprieve; he would be all right. He was immediately taken to Bellevue Hospital, where he was treated for multiple gunshot wounds. Against doctor's orders, he left the hospital to attend his sentencing for his sexual assault conviction, which was to be held the next day. Arriving in a wheelchair with a thick bandage around his head, Shakur was sentenced to 18 months for sexual assault, which he was to begin serving at Clinton Correctional Facility on February 14, 1995. A month later, Interscope released *Me against the World*, making Shakur the first—and only—artist in music history to have an album debut at no. 1 on the Billboard charts while in jail. It stayed in position for more than a month, with strong sales that were far higher than any other album out at the time. During the first week alone, the album sold 240,000 copies, making Shakur the top-selling solo male rap artist to hit such an achievement. Produced by Easy Mo Bee, Johnny J, and Tony Pizarro, the album is a favorite for many rap fans, and it was largely considered refreshing among the overexaggerated gangsta albums coming of the West Coast. In place of "hoes and bitches" were lyrics that explored the consequences of violence and the downfalls of organized crime.

While in jail, Shakur also delved into the writings of Sun Tzu and Niccolò Machiavelli, two writers that focused on political strategy as well as the philosophies behind those strategies. He wrote many poems as well as a screenplay titled *Live 2 Tell* and was isolated, for which he later blamed old friends, given that few people visited him while in jail, past his long-time girlfriend Keisha Morris and a small handful of reporters. He married Morris while in prison, though he annulled the marriage within weeks of his release.

As a result of efforts by his lawyer, Shakur's case was on appeal by October 1995, though he was unable to raise the $1.4 million needed for bail. Like a shark smelling blood, Death Row mogul Suge Knight visited Shakur in prison, offering to help fund his release if the rapper would sign to Death Row. Tired of prison and ready for life on the streets, Shakur agreed, and lawyer Kenner created a makeshift, three-record contract that was handwritten on paper found in Shakur's cell. Knight put up $250,000 toward the bail, with Interscope and MCA providing the rest of the money (Ro, 1999, p. 250).

"HIT 'EM UP"

Now with Death Row and back in California, Shakur immediately began working in the Can Am Studios, forming a new group called the Outlawz, which featured three New Jersey men who were previously known as Dramacydal. The group was featured on a few songs on Shakur's *Me Against the World*, and Shakur was eager to work with the men again. With the Outlawz, Shakur recorded his infamous "diss track" "Hit 'Em Up," a brutal assault on Wallace and the rest of the Bad Boy camp. In the song, he calls Wallace fat after claiming to have slept with Faith Evans, a claim he makes three times. He calls out several people by name, most notably Wallace, Lil' Cease, Lil' Kim, and Mobb Deep, claiming that those with Bad Boy are just trying to create drama and don't realize the serious situation they've started, given that they aren't really from the streets. But many made similar claims about Shakur, who, despite having grown up relatively poor, still did not have to hustle for a living and was never associated with gangs until after he rapped about being in one. Even so, Shakur began acting as if he were in a gang, claiming battle with Wallace, Combs, and the rest of the Bad Boy crew, igniting a war based wholly on his belief that Wallace had set him up at Quad Studios.

THE EAST COAST–WEST COAST RAP RIVALRY

At Death Row, Dre's *The Chronic* and Snoop's *Doggystyle* pushed their way to the forefront of mainstream music. As America's focus shifted to the left coast, many New York rappers saw their status—and profitability—diminish, finding themselves for the first time fighting their way to the top of the hill as West Coast rappers dominated both the charts and the airwaves. But with the release of *Ready to Die*, and with Shakur's newfound hatred of all things Wallace and Combs, the rivalry moved from one about a quest for listeners to a personal issue between Death Row and Bad Boy Records.

Bad Boy's popularity—and roster—grew, and so did animosity between the two coasts. In September 1995, one of Knight's closest friends, Jake Robeles, was gunned down at an after-party held after So So Def producer Jermaine Dupri's birthday bash in Atlanta. Both Knight and Combs were at the Platinum House when an argument erupted. Robeles was shot and killed, and Knight reportedly immediately blamed Combs for ordering a hit. Combs has always denied these charges.

"I'm not a gangsta, and I don't have no rivalry with no person in the industry whatsoever," Combs later said in an interview published in *Vibe*. "The whole shit is stupid, trying to make an East Coast/West Coast war. East Coast, West Coast, Death Row, Def Jam, or Uptown. I feel nothing but proud for anybody young and black and making money. [Some people] want us to be at each other, at war with each other" (Powell, 1996).

But the war Combs claimed not to want was already underway and was egged on by Shakur's public statements that Bad Boy was behind the Quad Studio shootings, accusations he felt were proved true by Wallace's single "Who Shot Ya," the b-side of Wallace's popular "Big Poppa." Despite knowing the song was recorded months before the shooting, Shakur felt that the song was an affront to him and that it proved Wallace planned the shooting in advance. Wallace always denied Shakur's charges, maintaining he had no idea Shakur would be held up and shot. But Shakur still insisted, and Knight, always one to fuel a fire, backed Shakur's claims, often egging on Shakur's bravado, bringing the once socially aware, intelligent rapper even further into the world of violence and gangs.

THE ROLE OF GANGS IN RAP

Gangs have been a prominent part of Southern California culture since the late 1960s and early 1970s, when two sects rose to infamy. Known as the Bloods and the Crips, both groups have deep clutches on the impoverished, depressed areas where crime and violence often offer more than an education and a legitimate job. The older of the two gangs, the Crips was started in 1969 by 15-year-old Raymond Washington, a young man who found role models within the political group the Black Panthers. Washington led a group of young men to commit acts of robbery and violence as a way to gain attention, getting their name from their use of canes during one of their first holdups. The victims—a group of Asian merchants—tried to describe to police their assailants, frustratingly shouting the word "Crip!" when not able to remember the English word for cane. A newspaper reporter overheard the exchange and named the gang Crips in the article. Through the years, the gang has abandoned its initial social agendas and has splintered into multiple factions largely determined by geographics (e.g., the Compton Crips).

The Bloods were formed in opposition to the Crips, previously having been loosely associated youth gangs that felt bullied by the Crips. Members of a gang known as the Mob Piru Boys called together all the non-Crips gangs, and an alliance was formed. Soon the Bloods outnumbered the Crips, and small wars on the streets of Los Angeles are still continually waged.

Much of the music coming out the West Coast claims some affiliation with either the Crips or the Bloods, something many argue is meant to boost album sales by establishing street credit through claiming crimes and a life that isn't necessarily true. Out of the most famous Death Row artists, only Snoop and Daz have gang affiliations, both with the Crips. DJ Quik is a noted member of the Mob Piru Bloods. But others have no real affiliation. For instance, despite being the father of gangsta rap, Dr. Dre has never been a part of any gang, having been raised in a relatively stable household. The same is true of Shakur, whose lyrics largely preceded his actual involvement in gang violence.

Perhaps the most notable instance of someone embracing the gangster lifestyle lies with Suge Knight, who has intertwined his life with the Bloods, even using the gang's trademark color—red—as an integral part of the Death Row logo. From day one, Knight publicly flaunted his affiliation with the Mob Piru Bloods, covering all furniture and cabinets at the Death Row offices in deep red, with the floor covered in a deep red carpet, save the outline of the label's logo. Members of the Bloods were allowed to have guns inside the studio, and Knight's German shepherd dog, always beside his master, was named Damu, Swahili for "blood." Legend has it the dog was trained to kill on Knight's command, though there is no record of a death inside the office.

Knight led Death Row as if it were a street gang, using violence to reprimand, as seen with rapper Lynwood Stanley and his brother George Stanley, two men who used a payphone reserved only for calls from the label's benefactor, Michael "Harry-O" Harris. Because Harris was in jail, he could call only at certain times, making the payphone off-limits to anyone except Knight. The brothers insisted on using the phone, telling

Knight they were guests of Dre. "By challenging Suge about the phone and also challenging Suge about his authority, they just found themselves in an awkward position" (Ro, 1999, p. 85).

According to several sources, Knight stripped and beat the two men, leaving them only to go down to his car to grab a gun he kept hidden under the seat. Once back upstairs, Knight fired at least one shot, lodging a bullet in the wall behind the men. He then used the gun to pistol-whip Lynwood Stanley, stopping only after repeated requests from several others. Sources report that he then took Stanley's wallet, telling him that if he went to authorities, Knight would seek retribution. His warning didn't work, and the brothers did, in fact, file a complaint against Knight, leading to a raid on the Death Row studios. Knight was apprehended and charged, though the case would later result in nothing more than a suspended sentence and probation, which Knight repeatedly violated (Ro, 1999, p. 85).

Such acts of violence were common at the Death Row offices, where gang members—both Crips and Bloods—acted as security alongside off-duty LAPD officers, all armed and contributing to a rather intimidating atmosphere for many outside the label who stopped by to visit. In the carpet of Knight's office was Death Row's logo, and his office walls were painted red, a color Knight almost always wore during photo shoots. In Las Vegas, Knight painted red the walls of his pool, a color that faded to orange as the chlorine and hot Vegas sun bleached the once-deep hue. He also named his bar Club 662, the word "MOB" as it is spelled on a phone pad, which many believe stood for "Member of Bloods," meaning he officially pledged allegiance to the deadly street gang.

As for Combs, according to some sources, he had several connections to the Gambino Mafia Family, his closest connection being with the family's "enforcer" Andrew Campos, who attended the private Roman Catholic high school Mount St. Michael Academy in the Bronx. The two played together on the football team and were apparently good friends while in school. Many claim that Campos and his fellow gang members attended several recording sessions with Wallace and Combs, sparking Wallace's initial inkling to call his debut album *The Teflon Don*, in honor of John Gotti, head of the Gambino crime family.

MENTORING OTHER RAPPERS

Introduced in a shout-out on Wallace's first single "Party and Bullshit," Junior M.A.F.I.A. came from the same neighborhood from which Wallace once came up. Junior M.A.F.I.A. featured rappers Lil' Ceasar, Chico Delvac, Nino Brown, Larceny, Trife, MC Klepto, and Lil' Kim, all from Bedford-Stuyvesant. Wallace, having known everyone since they were all young children, had a special friendship with rappers Chico Delvac and Lil' Cease. Chico was the one who first introduced Wallace to the streets that would become Wallace's bread and butter, first while selling crack and later through sales of albums telling of his days as a hustler. Cease was there for Wallace when he first started to hit it big, often playing errand boy, retrieving sodas and weed for the older Wallace. Having met Wallace at Brooklyn's Fulton Mall in the early 1990s Lil' Kim was always someone in Wallace's life; the two had on-again, off-again affairs from their teen years to his death, and Kim even tattooed his name on her body, much like Wallace's wife would later do.

Originally just a name the group threw around sometimes while clowning on the streets, killing time between hustles, Junior M.A.F.I.A. became a reality as soon as Wallace said their name at the end of his remix, making what had just been an idea now a reality. Almost as soon as *Ready to Die* was released, Wallace looked toward developing the group more, bringing in old friend Lance "Understanding" Rivera to help.

Rivera came from those same streets and was a heavy-set, hustler-minded man who grasped not only what it took to survive but also what it took to succeed. Always interested in the music industry, Rivera didn't actively seek a role in Wallace's life until after Combs snubbed him at a video shoot for *Ready to Die*, when he was visiting Wallace, a longtime friend. Rivera later said it was that snubbing that made him want to show Combs he could be a formidable opponent. It was Rivera's brother Justice who reportedly first realized Wallace's potential, often handing off his mix tapes to other musicians, with one eventually landing in the hands of Mister Cee. Rivera often loaned Wallace money, when he was broke just before *Ready to Die* hit the streets. Once Wallace hit it big, though, the two formed the small company on which they would release Junior M.A.F.I.A. Eventually, Rivera and Combs became friends, working together on Lil' Kim's debut.

"Puffy was an element of what Biggie was," said Rivera. "I influenced what Biggie rapped about, Puffy did the music and Biggie was the artist. That was the key. So now I'm bringing that key to Lil' Cease and Lil' Kim. It'll be Me, Cease and Puff, and Me, Kim and Puff. It was Undeas and it was Bad Boy. Together we stood victorious, and we're going to continue to do that" (Mukherjee, 1998).

Wallace and Rivera soon produced and released Junior M.A.F.I.A.'s debut album, *Conspiracy*, under the Undeas label. The album debuted at no. 8 on the Billboard 200 charts and was certified gold within weeks of its debut, as was its main single, "Player's Anthem." The album's second single, "Get Money," featured Wallace and Lil' Kim in a duet that not only helped launch Lil' Kim's successful solo career but also fueled rumors the two were secretly dating, despite his marriage to Faith Evans.

Chapter 5

MO MONEY, MO PROBLEMS

Despite his commercial success, Wallace's personal life was falling apart, with his frequent affairs continually incensing Evans. Her jealousy surfaced on many occasions, and she once went after a groupie who had answered Wallace's phone the night before. Immediately upon hearing the woman's voice, Evans had asked a friend to watch her daughter and caught a flight to Virginia to confront Wallace and the woman. As soon as Wallace's hotel room door opened, Evans attacked the woman inside, punching her face and kicking her in the stomach until Wallace pulled his wife off the unknown woman, who was fully dressed at the time. Evans screamed at Wallace before leaving, headed for the airport where she caught a flight back to New York. Despite having a handful of shows left on tour, Wallace followed his wife back to Brooklyn, asking around until he finally found her. Although she was still angry at first, eventually the two reconciled and were again fine (Coker, 2003, p. 165).

In May 1995, Wallace got into a fight with a Camden, New Jersey, club promoter, ending in a later arrest. After playing Club Xscape, Wallace received only half of the $20,000 promised, and the rapper sought out promoter Brook Herdell for the rest of his fee.

Wallace allegedly forced the promoter's driver, Nathaniel Banks Jr., to take him to Herdell's home. But once outside Herdell's house, Banks and Wallace got into a fistfight, and Banks claimed Wallace robbed him of a necklace, bracelet, watch, cell, and a few hundred dollars. Wallace maintained he wasn't the one who attacked Banks, although the Camden police issued a warrant for his arrest, based on Banks's allegations. Police mistakenly sent the documents to Wallace's old address, 226 St. James

Place, and because he was actively touring, he never received the information and didn't know to turn himself in. A high-profile man, Wallace was well known in many cities he visited, and police were easily able to track the rapper down, as they did six weeks later at a show in Philadelphia. Wallace was not expecting the cops who were waiting for him as soon as the show at Pulsations was over. Their guns pulled, officers forced Wallace to the ground, shouting his Miranda rights, and one officer even asked him for an autograph, saying his daughter loved Wallace's music. He spent three days in jail, crying and vomiting, worried that he would be kept in prison. He didn't want to be there. He couldn't go back to jail.

Wallace felt he had more to lose than ever before—a wife, his daughter, and his success. Though he hadn't spent much time with the young T'Yanna, he wanted to know his child better and to see her more often. He was building a house for his mom in the Poconos and purchasing one for himself and Evans in Teaneck, New Jersey. Wallace felt the new, large New Jersey house would reflect his new wealth, demonstrating how he'd grown as a person. "To me, if you stay in the same spot as you were in when you were doing nothing, and now you're doing something, that's not progression," Wallace told *New York Times* reporter Charisse Jones. "You don't want to deal with subways and gunshots. You want to be comfortable and safe" (Jones, 1995).

But even though the move may have made him feel safe, he wouldn't stay comfortable because the cost of his life far outshined his income. With the multiple cars and homes, as well as his mounting living expenses, Wallace was broke, spending money far faster than he received it. He still hadn't profited from *Ready to Die* because the costs of the album had not yet been recouped. Notorious for his slow recording process and love of expensive marijuana, Wallace spent hours in the expensive Manhattan studios, often just drinking with the other musicians. Add in the money Combs paid to Uptown for Wallace's earlier tracks, and it would be some time before Wallace saw a paycheck. Strapped for cash, Wallace sold the publishing rights to his songs to Combs for only $250,000, rights that would later prove to be worth tens of millions.

At the time, Wallace shrugged off the purchase, claiming that signing a few papers was worth getting a quarter-million dollars. But the money didn't last long, given that it barely covered his past-due bills then. His mother had always told him to save for a rainy day. And even though he was a top-selling rapper whose songs played on every corner, Wallace was praying the clouds wouldn't come.

And financially, they stayed away, though his personal life was slowly falling apart, starting first with his marriage. Although she was never a particularly jealous woman, Faith Evans wasn't one to look the other way. As she and her husband became more famous, Evans learned more about her husband's life, suffering through the countless radio comments and gossip that connected Wallace to other women, such as rappers Charli Baltimore and Lil' Kim.

It was Kim who seemed to bother Evans the most because the petite firecracker had recently taken to talking publicly about Wallace and Evans, claiming the two had broken up and that it was a fact of which she had intimate knowledge. Kim and Wallace went back several years, a few before he met Evans, and his wife always suspected the two had something going. And as they both continued to work on their own careers, spending far more time apart than together, it became increasingly clear their marriage wasn't working.

Evans and Wallace officially separated, and she left for Los Angeles to attend the release party for the soundtrack to *Waiting to Exhale*, a drama starring Whitney Houston and Angela Bassett. Evans's song "Kissing You" was featured in the movie and on the soundtrack, her first such soundtrack debut. At an after-party, she ran into her old friend Treach, a rapper with the popular group Naughty by Nature. Through Treach she met Shakur. The two posed for several pictures, and Shakur bought Evans several drinks, all the while talking about possible collaborations. She agreed, thinking the exposure would be good for her career. She later swore she didn't know that Shakur and Wallace had a rivalry because she and Wallace were no longer speaking.

The night progressed, and not long after midnight, Shakur asked if she'd like to go back to the studio and lay down some vocals for their collaborations. She agreed. Shakur brought her back to the CAN-AM studios, where they worked for a short time. Evans had never been to the Death Row studios before and later said that it was intimidating, with armed men everywhere, and that the whole place had a bad vibe. The two didn't stay long, and she left after Shakur assured her he would add his part later.

Within a month, Shakur began telling people he had slept with Evans, making comments on radio shows and in conversations with reporters. In one such conversation, Shakur slyly responded, "I never kiss and tell," though he had claimed several times to have slept with her. In a *New York Times Magazine* article on Suge Knight, writer Lynn Hirschberg described the following scene:

> The rest of the Death Row posse were wearing red and black
> ... Shakur is the only one in a different color: he's wearing an
> elaborately patterned gold shirt and baggy jeans. "The wife of

a top rapper bought this for him," Suge says, razzing Tupac. "Who's that?" Tupac smiles. "His name is an acronym." Suge smiles. "Notorious B.I.G.'s wife, Faith Evans."

Tupac nods.... "She bought him this and a suit and some other stuff," Knight says. "And how did you thank her, Tupac?" Tupac pauses. "I did enough," he says, rather salaciously. (Hirschberg, 1996)

Evans has always denied sleeping with Shakur, as well his claims of her buying him a suit. Shakur always insisted he did sleep with Evans. Wallace apparently cast off the rumors for a while until it became too much. In February 1996, Wallace immediately caught a plane to confront Evans, heading straight for her hotel room, where he banged on the door and yelled in the hall until she finally let him in. Once inside, he pushed her against the wall, keeping her pinned until he finally accepted what she continually told him—she had not had sex with Shakur. But during their argument, Evans had a few questions of her own. Was he sleeping with Lil' Kim? After denying it for a few minutes, he finally admitted his and Kim's relationship. She told him to leave, and he soon did. She later had the tattoo reading "B.I.G." changed to "B.I.G. Fay," an act of rebellion against her husband (Coker, 2003).

Though they were separated, the two didn't discuss divorce. They didn't discuss much at all, actually, until Evans soon called Wallace to tell him she was pregnant with his child. He reportedly never asked if the baby was Shakur's, though he later joked about it on wax (on a record). In Jay-Z's debut *Reasonable Doubts*, Wallace rapped about his wife's pregnancy and the possibility of her having had slept with Shakur on the song "Brooklyn's Finest": "If Faith has twins, she'll probably have two Pacs. Get it? Tu ... Pac's." Wallace later told a reporter he made the joke about the pregnancy because he felt the whole situation was ridiculous because the allegation was completely untrue. Besides that, he said, he didn't have it in his nature to hate others, especially an old friend. Wallace told the reporter he had asked his wife at the time if she had sleep with Shakur, and she told him no. He accepted her word, choosing to believe his wife rather than question her for the rest of their relationship ("Stakes Is High," 1996).

Though he remained tight-lipped about it, Wallace told several friends he would happily make amends with his old friend, a man he hadn't seen in several months. Shakur, though, did not seem ready to make nice; he continually brought up Wallace in interviews, always pledging his allegiance to the West Coast. Fans across the country often claimed to be behind either Wallace or Shakur, their loyalty lying either with East Coast or West Coast, and the debate became almost a novelty among mainstream music and was frequent in white suburban America, with many using gang signs meant to symbolize their affiliation with one of the two coasts. It seemed almost everyone was talking about it, with one exception: Wallace himself. The rapper remained notoriously quiet on the topic of Shakur, with his appearance on Jay-Z's song being one of the only times he mentioned his old friend.

But soon, the war would claim the life of the friend whom many felt was the only one who could bring Wallace and Shakur back together: Randy "Stretch" Walker. He and Shakur had started Thug Life and were close friends for years. Walker also knew Wallace, and the three men had once recorded a song together for *Ready to Die*, though Combs had later scrapped the track, something that had always bothered Shakur.

Exactly one year to the day from the Quad Studios shooting, Wallace and Shakur's shared friend Randy "Stretch" Walker was killed after an unknown assailant in a black Acura followed his SUV, shooting at him with a high-powered rifle. Walker's SUV flipped and crashed, and the gunman from the Acura fired shots into the SUV before fleeing the scene. The three had been close friends for several years, though their relationship had deteriorated after Shakur's shooting. Depending on whom you asked, his murder was considered a warning to either coast. Perhaps to those on the West Coast, his death meant that the East Coast still ruled their territory, no matter what Knight and the artists at his label might have thought. Or perhaps for those on the East Coast, it was meant as retaliation for the Quad Studios shooting and as a warning to never try such a hit again. Both Wallace and Shakur took Walker's death personally, though neither confronted the other about it.

And in the end, his death had neither of the two supposed meanings. According to papers filed in federal court in April 2007, Ronald "Tenad" Washington and other gang-bangers from the Queens-based Hollis Crew shot and killed Walker in a case of mistaken identity, thinking that Walker was Washington's own brother, whom they meant to kill. The facts came out during testimony surrounding Washington's confession to the 2002 murder of Jason Mizell, better known as Run D.M.C.'s Jam Master Jay, an iconic DJ whose contributions to hip-hop are almost unparalleled. He was shot and killed during a robbery at a recording studio in Queens's Jamaica neighborhood.

THE RIVALRY HEATS UP

At the 1995 Source Awards held in New York, Knight brought the feud to televised attention after announcing on stage, "If you don't want the owner of your label on your album or in your video or on your tour, come sign with Death Row." Soon after Knight's announcement, Combs tried to settle any dispute in his own speech. "Contrary to what other people may feel, I would like to say that I am very proud of Dr. Dre, of Death Row and Suge Knight for their accomplishments and all this East and West needs to stop," he said (Ro, 1999, p. 227).

It didn't help. The crowd, already against both the West Coast and Death Row, were incensed, booing once Snoop and Dre took the stage to perform a song. "The East Coast ain't got no love for Dr. Dre and Snoop Dogg?" Snoop said. "Ya'll don't love us?" His tone was incredulous while also bearing a tone of confrontation, and the crowd answered back with boos, some standing, their hands waving downward (Ro, 1998, p. 227).

Most award shows featuring the two groups displayed similar animosities, including the 1996 MTV Awards as well as that year's Soul Train Awards, held in Los Angeles. There Wallace and Shakur saw each other for the first time since the 1994 shooting at Quad Studios, and it was also the first time the two had interacted since Shakur spread word he had slept with Faith Evans, regardless of whether it was true. The Bad Boy group was there largely in support of Evans, who was nominated for two awards, as well as Wallace, who was also nominated for an award, as was Shakur. Regardless of the accolades they received onstage, both groups were ready for a showdown backstage. Writer Ronin Ro later described the scene as similar to a Western—guns were drawn, and "both camps circled each other like prey" (Ro, 1999, p. 282). There, Ro writes, Wallace realized that his former friend Shakur was no longer the man he had known before, having now taken to movie-like violence to solve problems.

Despite the animosity, the showdown ended without violence, though the rivalry flourished, becoming more heated as Death Row announced the opening of a new office called Death Row East, which was to be head-quartered in New York City. Running full-page ads in several hip-hop magazines, the label claimed to have signed former Bad Boy artist Craig Mack, though Mack now claims he never signed to Death Row. He never released anything through the label, though he did rather abruptly cut ties with Bad Boy around the time of the advertisements.

Magazines like *The Source* and *Vibe* heavily covered the rivalry, frequently featuring articles about both camps. The controversy became one of Death Row's prevailing assets and was heavily marketed, almost more so than the music. This was one of the main reasons Dre decided to leave Death Row, choosing to forgo his rights to the master tapes as well as his half of the company in lieu of a calmer, more productive atmosphere at his new venture, Aftermath Entertainment. His exit seemed only to anger Shakur, who added the producer to the growing list of artists he mocked in songs.

Many outside the rivalry found it not only annoying but also damaging to the headway both Combs and Knight had made in the music industry, both climbing ladders that had never existed before. Combs had been barely old enough to drink when he formed what has become one of the most profitable record labels in history. Knight forged a path that didn't exist before, creating a solid backdrop to what were some of the most influential releases that reshaped popular music.

"I'm ready for [this beef] to come to a head, however it gotta go down," Combs said in a 1996 *Vibe* interview. "I'm ready for it to be out of my life and be over with. I mean that from the bottom of my heart. I just hope it can end quick and in a positive way, because it's gotten out of hand" ("Stakes Is High," 1996).

MORE ARRESTS, MORE PROBLEMS

On March 23, 1996, Wallace and Damien "D-Roc" Butler were arrested after a Faith Evans concert at New York City's Palladium after the pair confronted two loud and argumentative fans. The show was late ending, and Wallace and Butler didn't see the fans until just before 4:30 A.M., when they hailed a cab to follow the cab the pair themselves had just hailed. Just a few blocks up, at the intersection of Union Square and 16th Street, Wallace and Butler jumped out of their cab and rushed the other taxi, smashing its windows with baseball bats while yelling at the fans inside. They were almost immediately arrested. A few days later—and still out on bail—Wallace, Money L, and Lil' Cease were smoking a blunt outside Brooklyn's Fulton Mall when they were arrested. Finally, just a few weeks after that, police came to Wallace's Teaneck home after receiving complaints of an illegally parked car just beside Wallace's drive. Officers came to the door to ask the driver of the car—rapper Mase—to move his vehicle. The police smelled marijuana smoke and immediately left, returning a short while later with a search warrant. Officers found a huge bag of weed and four semiautomatics with filed-off serial numbers. Lil' Cease and Wallace were arrested.

SHAKUR KILLED

Soon Shakur began to step away from Death Row, telling friends he instead wanted to focus on more positive creative outlets, such as making movies and creating a small company called Euphanasia to receive scripts.

By the summer of 1996, Shakur had begun to make the change, having more than enough songs to complete the last of his three-album obligation to Death Row, freeing him to talk to other labels, including Warner Brothers, who expressed interest in signing the rapper. Shakur also had two movies slated to hit theaters, and he wanted to take advantage of the press surrounding those releases to land more roles. He and his girlfriend Kidada Jones, Quincy Jones's daughter, were talking of having children. He also was talking about funding sports teams and a children's center in South Central Los Angeles (Ro, 1999, p. 291).

Ultimately, though, Shakur just wanted to leave Death Row, an increasingly negative place filled with violence and secrecy. Shakur already questioned Death Row's money practices, having not seen any money from the sales of *All Eyez on Me*, a multiplatinum hit. Shakur continued to ask Death Row lawyer David Kenner, his financial representative, for his money until he was finally told he owed nearly $5 million to the label for expenses and recording costs, a number that seemed impossible with such high sales. Shakur almost instantly fired Kenner as his attorney, a move that some around him—including other rappers on the Death Row label, sources later reported—saw as dangerous, given that Kenner was so closely tied with Knight, who was still battling several assault charges in court. There was no evidence that Shakur feared Knight, but the exit of several others on the Death Row roster—including cofounder Dr. Dre—did not come without controversy and rumors of threatened violence. By firing Kenner, Shakur was starting the separation between himself and Death Row, solidifying his move toward independence. Past that, Shakur kept his plans for the future to himself, knowing how Knight had reacted when others—such as Dre and former Death Row artist Sam Sneed—left the label. In keeping with appearances, he decided to join Knight and the rest of the Death Row group at a Mike Tyson–Bruce Sheldon fight at the MGM Grand in Las Vegas on September 7, 1996. He expressed his misgivings about attending the fight to Kidada Jones, who asked him to wear a bullet-resistant vest. He refused, claiming it would be too hot. He left with Knight, unprotected.

The Tyson–Sheldon fight ended in a quick knockout, and the Death Row entourage left the arena, headed for a party at Knight's Club 662. In the MGM lobby, Shakur, Knight, and the others encountered Orlando "Baby Lane" Jones, a well-known Crip involved with stealing a Death Row gold chain earlier that year.

Knight, Shakur, and the rest of the Death Row entourage attacked Jones, kicking and pummeling him in a display caught on the MGM's gritty black and white security cameras. But as quickly as the fight had begun, it ended, and the group rushed for the exit. Shakur returned to his room at the Luxor, where he changed before quickly leaving again.

The group met at Knight's house, where they piled into cars, headed for Knight's club, where Run D.M.C. were playing. Knight and Shakur were at the helm of the convoy in Knight's black BMW, with Knight at the wheel. At least seven cars were following the group, including a car filled with the off-duty Los Angeles Police Department officers Knight employed as security.

The lengthy convoy stopped at a traffic light at the intersection of East Flamingo Road and Koval Lane, just a block off the Vegas strip. A white Cadillac with California plates pulled beside the BMW, its driver-side window just an arm's length away from Shakur. A hand extended toward the BMW, and in it was a black gun, most likely a revolver. At least 10 shots were fired, the car glass shattering as the many fans standing on the sidewalk screamed, some having just a minute before taken pictures of the popular rapper. Desperate to escape the bullets, Shakur scrambled for the backseat, though not quickly enough. Bullets tore into his slender body, two in his lower chest, inside his "Thug Life" tattoo, a third hitting his leg, and a fourth hitting his thigh. Slivers of glass pierced his skin, slashing his head and face. He lay in the backseat, his breathing heavily labored as Knight hit the gas, pulling from the intersection despite two flat tires and a shattered windshield. They didn't get far. Within just a few blocks, police and an ambulance were behind them. Authorities took both men to the hospital, and Knight was treated for only minor scrapes, despite his initial claims of being shot in his head. Once treated, though, he reportedly left without saying anything to the group waiting, which included Mike Tyson, actress Jasmine Guy, the Rev. Jesse Jackson, and Shakur's mother, Afeni Shakur, all waiting to hear if Shakur had survived the bullets.

And Shakur was alive, despite a considerable loss of blood and the loss of one lung. Doctors expected him to recover, though it would be a slow recovery. Fans and reporters crowded the parking lot, holding vigils as police watched for outbreaks of gang-related violence. Instead the gathered crowd was devastated and distraught over Shakur's shooting and had little interest in fighting each other.

Back in Los Angeles at the Death Row offices, publicist George Pryce worked extra hours handling the crisis as Death Row artist Nate Dogg finished recording his album *Christmas on Death Row*. "We need help bad," Dogg told reporter Ronin Ro. "That's my feeling. We run around killing ... shooting all them people that's our same color." Dogg said he felt that in an atmosphere where many young black men are either killed in gang-related violence or imprisoned, many lose hope and end up contributing to the violence themselves. "Only comment at this time I can say about anything is pray for Tupac. That's about it. The rest of it don't seem to make no sense right now" (Ro, 1999, p. 297). But no sentiments were able to help Shakur. On September 13, 1996, just before 4 P.M., doctors pronounced Tupac Shakur dead from respiratory failure and cardiopulmonary arrest resulting from the gunshots. He was 25.

Almost instantly, his death sparked a gang battle throughout Los Angeles, an onslaught that claimed the lives of dozens of Bloods and Crips who fought for little more than their association with particular gangs.

After Shakur's death, Wallace called Evans, crying. She felt that he was scared he was next and that he was upset his friend had died without their ever reconciling. But almost as soon as Shakur was killed, the rumors began, and Wallace's name was almost always mentioned in connection, whether the news source was MTV, BET, or CNN. In newspapers, the East–West feud was thoroughly explored, and without question, many signs pointed to Wallace.

Though he rarely spoke publicly about Shakur's death, Wallace was reportedly rather shaken, having hoped the two would reconcile as Shakur distanced himself from Death Row. But as it stood, they would be immortalized as enemies, and according to a later news article as well as countless rumors and speculation, Wallace would be suspected for having ordered his former friend's death. He always insisted he had no role in Shakur's murder.

And as time passed, and after Shakur was buried, some began exploring other suspects, most of all Suge Knight. Now, the press viewed Knight as the symbolic triggerman, often mentioning his name in connection with the murder or outright accusing him of having orchestrated Shakur's death; they presented him as a mogul who ordered the death of his hottest rapper simply because he wanted to leave Death Row behind and because Knight wanted to hold onto Shakur and his monetary potential. For others, Wallace will forever be to blame, though the rapper himself soon saw hard times.

At the time, Knight's behavior was rather suspicious, according to several sources. Despite being told by police to remain on the scene, Knight immediately left the hospital after finding out Shakur wasn't initially dead. Las Vegas police were soon looking for the mogul but were unable to find him, and within a day of Shakur's shooting, police discovered Knight at the Death Row offices. Attorney David Kenner told authorities Knight would immediately return to Vegas for questioning, though he didn't arrive until two days later. At the Las Vegas Police headquarters,

Knight was reportedly difficult to work with, refusing to answer most questions. The only information he willingly offered was his belief that Crips were behind the shooting, despite a lack of proof. Knight also continually declared himself a victim of the shooting, claiming he was shot in the head. But the only injuries he sustained were minor cuts, not a massive gunshot. Within two days of Knight's interview, Shakur was dead. Despite having claimed Shakur as one of his closest friends, Knight only briefly stopped at the hospital, offering a quick condolence to Shakur's family before leaving (Sullivan, 2002, pp. 188–195).

WRECKED

Four days after Shakur's death, Wallace, his girlfriend Charli Baltimore, and Lil' Cease went to a New Jersey Lexus dealership, where one of Wallace's cars was being repaired, but the car wasn't quite ready yet. The dealership lent Wallace a Dodge Astrovan, and Lil' Cease climbed behind the wheel because Wallace still didn't drive, having never learned, common among many who grow up in the city.

Heavy rains made the highway wet, and Cease, as usual, drove fast and then lost control on a turn, the car weaving in his lane as Cease struggled to regain control. He never did, and the vehicle crossed the median, narrowly missing oncoming traffic as the car slid into a ditch. Cease lifted his head from the steering wheel, his front teeth falling into his lap as he looked over at Wallace, whose large size left him trapped between the seat and the dashboard. Wallace knew he was hurt, though at the time he wasn't quite sure how bad. In the backseat, blood flowed freely down Baltimore's face, her neck and leg both hurt.

Authorities soon arrived and had to use the Jaws of Life to cut Wallace out of the car, placing him on a stretcher. Once at the hospital, doctors delivered the news. Along with several scrapes and cuts, one of his thighbones was shattered. There was a chance he'd never walk again, and if he did, he'd likely always require a cane. He would have to undergo extensive rehabilitation and would need to stay in the hospital for weeks, if not months.

Wallace soon moved into a room at the Kessler Institute of Rehabilitation, where he spent his time recuperating in the same room in which Christopher Reeve convalesced after a tragic horse riding accident that left him paralyzed in May 1995. Wallace spent pivotal moments in this room, with formidable challenges lying ahead. Wallace—an overweight man who sometimes didn't want to walk more than a block—would now have to work hard to regain even the most basic use of his leg. He was also supposed to be working on his album, one that Combs and the others had traveled down to Trinidad to record, one that would restore him back as one of the East Coast's top rappers, a honor he knew was slipping.

But although at first the odds seemed daunting, Wallace soon found himself enjoying the first taste of a sober quiet he'd had in years. So much had happened in such a short time—it had been just a few years since he had been hawking crack on the corner of St. James Place and Fulton Street in Brooklyn, and now he was a rap star, with one of his friends dead in a murder many felt was his fault, and two coasts were pitted against each other in a war that was now real. His wife had left him because of his infidelity and, angry at his affairs, had fought one of his girlfriends—Lil' Kim—at Combs's studio, punching the rapper several times in the face before being pulled off the smaller girl. Evans was pregnant with his second child, a boy who would be born in less than a month, and he barely knew the daughter he already had, having spent so much of his time touring and in the studio. Before, he had been ready to die, but now, having faced death, he was looking toward life after death.

Within weeks, Wallace was back in the studio, taking short leaves from his recuperation at Kessler to record an album he felt would far outshine *Ready to Die*. He was older now, more mature, and was ready to explore themes he hadn't touched before, ones that dipped deep into the new style of rap coming up in the East. Called mafioso, the style indulged the fantasies of rappers by letting them imagine themselves as heavies in organized crime, often referencing movies or actual crime families. In Combs's studio, Daddy's House, workers had things ready for Wallace—the weed rolled into a blunt, the Hennessey opened—and though he first returned in a wheelchair, Wallace was in full game, laughing and talking to old friends before laying down lyrics that were as clever as they were captivating, often leaving the room speechless. Wallace became the narrator and star in a world he created, a world he felt would return him to his throne as King of New York.

Notorious B.I.G., who won rap artist and rap single of the year, clutches his awards at the podium during the Billboard Music Awards in New York on the evening of December 6, 1995. Courtesy AP Photos/Mark Lennihan.

Rap star Christopher Wallace, aka Notorious B.I.G., walks to a waiting police car outside the 6th Police Precinct in the borough of Manhattan on Saturday, March 23, 1996 in New York. Wallace was arrested earlier that day after he and a friend used baseball bats to attack two fans who had asked the performer for his autograph, according to police. Courtesy AP Photos/Adam Nadel.

Lil' Kim, right, is escorted by Mary J. Blige following the funeral for Notorious B.I.G. at the Frank E. Campbell Funeral Home in New York, Tuesday, March 18, 1997. Courtesy AP Photos/ Adam Nadel.

An unidentified neighbor of Notorious B.I.G., top right, watches the funeral procession pass as mourners line the streets near the building where the slain rapper once lived on St. James Place in the Brooklyn borough of New York, Tuesday, March 18, 1997. Courtesy AP Photos/Mark Lennihan.

This is a detailed composite sketch that Los Angeles police released Thursday, March 27, 1997, of the suspect they say gunned down Notorious B.I.G. earlier that month in Los Angeles. Courtesy AP Photos/Los Angeles Police.

Chapter 6

SKY'S THE LIMIT

But before he could once again rule New York, Wallace first needed to take over Los Angeles because Combs and Wallace agreed that the West Coast–East Coast feud had severely damaged his popularity in California. In the East, Combs already had the press kicking with several feature stories planned for a few high-profile magazines, including *Spin*. Wallace wanted to undo some of the damage he felt was inflicted by the excessive wealth depicted in his videos as well as the inherent violence of the rap rivalry, an animosity that turned off many other East Coast rappers.

In several interviews, Wallace mentioned some of the hate that he felt came from his own neighborhood as well as others in the industry. In fact, some aspects of Bad Boy were often criticized, such as Combs's heavy-handed samples as well as the depiction of their lives in videos, as was parodied in The Root's video "What They Do," which cleverly presents itself as a "Rap Video Manual" and mocks many of the elements now common in rap videos, such as scantily-clad dancing girls, popped bottles of champagne, club scenes, and several shots of rappers "keeping it real" on the streets. The lyrics give away the intent of their video: "The principles of true hip-hop have been forsaken." The Roots felt that much of hip-hop was now focused on money, a theme that was increasingly prevalent, with the budget of a single hip-hop video rivaling that of an inner-city school, all the while showcasing a lifestyle that was largely rooted in superficial gain, with the fancy cars, big houses, and beautiful women who were often no more than props.

But for Wallace, this video depicted the life he felt he deserved, a sentiment he often expressed in interviews, because he felt he had paid his due on the streets and now deserved to revel in the bounty of top album sales, sold-out shows, and the scores of women who often offered themselves to Wallace, a sharp divergence from his attitude just a few years earlier, when he had told several reporters that he wouldn't be the man he was without the streets and that he felt an obligation to his fans to remain as rooted in that poverty-stricken reality as he could, even if it was in address and attitude only.

Still, though, he felt the album *Life after Death* reflected a growth that did come from his success, something he felt the fans would understand. As he told a *Vibe* reporter who interviewed him less than a month before his death, "I call this album *Life After Death* because when I was writing [the angry lyrics for *Ready to Die*]...I was dead. There was nothing but anger coming out about everything, about having to go out to sell crack, to hustle for a living, nothing but anger. But now I can't do that anymore. People know that Biggie ain't on the corner selling drugs no more" (Coker, 2003, p. 213).

Combs, ever the marketer, knew that much of the extravagance Wallace displayed in his videos, in interviews, and in pictures was beginning to backfire because it had been more than two years since he had had a new album, and many critics were beginning to wonder if he could deliver another *Ready to Die*. Wallace was eager to prove he could, happily answering interviewers' questions about the album, his style, and what he could still bring to the game.

But the hurdles he faced were often menacing, as Shakur still held a strong fan base in California, one that seemed almost impossible for Wallace to now penetrate. But the unofficial king of Los Angeles, Suge Knight, was now imprisoned, something many felt opened up the possibility for a reconciliation of coasts.

Knight returned to jail after the Las Vegas incident with Orlando Anderson, when a security camera caught on tape Knight delivering a few blows to Anderson. Despite Anderson's attempts on the stand to defend Knight, claiming the mogul tried to stop the fight, not encourage it, presiding judge Stephen Czuleger was not interested in hearing defenses of Knight. He was the same judge that had originally offered Knight a nine-year suspended sentence if he was to spend a month in a halfway house, not knowing at the time that that case's plaintiffs, the Stanley brothers, had recently signed a $1 million contract with Death Row or that the prosecutor's daughter, 18-year-old Gina Longo, had also recently signed to the label.

But Knight's ability to buy his freedom was muted once he kicked Orlando Anderson. There were no more plea bargains to be made. As his case concluded, and Knight was given the opportunity to speak on his behalf, he addressed the court in a rambling spiel that spanned topics from Afeni Shakur's request for her son's money to a list of the many reasons he shouldn't be jailed to his benevolence toward Anderson in how he didn't kick him but instead tried to help him, something the security cameras in the lobby of the MGM Grand didn't show. But Judge Stephen Czuleger said, "You really had everything going for you. You blew it" ("Rap's Stormy Knight," 2001).

But with Knight in jail, many felt that the tensions between the Bad Boy group and the dissipating Death Row group were falling, and there weren't the same problems anymore as there once were. Combs and Wallace constantly hit the streets, giving radio interviews and attending sporting events and shows, all meaning to show their love for California. Combs appeared with Snoop Doggy Dogg on *The Steve Harvey Show,* a move many thought would ease the issues between everyone, as the pair declared the long-standing bicoastal feud as over. But even with the high-profile interviews, both Combs and Wallace frequently received warnings from others who said they were overstaying their welcome. One such caution came from a bouncer at a club, who said they shouldn't forget that Knight still owned Los Angeles. Another warning came from basketball player Shaquille O'Neal, with whom Wallace had once recorded a track. The two ran into each other just after Wallace got his tattoo, and O'Neal made a point of telling the rapper of the dangers Los Angeles could pose.

And though they knew bad times could come, their trip was at first rather successful; they attended many parties and showed up at various clubs, even when they knew they weren't necessarily welcome. Wallace's manager Mark Pitts once told a reporter of such a moment, when several of Shakur's friends told Wallace they felt certain he had played a role in the rapper's death, wanting to retaliate for Shakur's having possibly slept with Evans. Pitts said Wallace fell back on his infamous charm, telling the men, "You know you love me, stop playing," instantly dissipating a potentially dangerous scene and turning it into one of the more fun nights they had in Los Angeles.

And because of moments like that, Wallace felt certain he could win back any audiences he may have lost. He told reporters he now looked toward the future, a future he felt was filled with the promise of wealth, health, and stability. Wallace wanted to open a line of restaurants he'd call Big Poppa's Chicken and Waffles, as well as continue working with his friend Lance "Un" Rivera to release records. He wanted to work more with Junior M.A.F.I.A., bringing in other artists as he saw fit and eventually building his own small music empire. He also wanted to work more with the clothing line he'd played around with some, one called Brooklyn

Mint. Wallace and Heavy D had talked about opening a line of clothing stores they'd call "Big and Heavy," which would feature the top-of-the-line plus-sized clothes he often wore in his videos. He also wanted to take a more active role in his children's lives, something he expressed in several interviews while out in California.

Wallace and Combs also dedicated a bit of time to Combs' first solo album, spending long nights in the studio. As when he had taken his Hit-men, a group of producers, to Trinidad to record *Life after Death*, Combs yet again longed for a fresh perspective, choosing this time the sunny West Coast. Combs and Wallace were also in Los Angeles to shoot the video for "Hypnotize," which would soon prove to be the last video Wallace was ever in, given that he died less than a month after filming. Directed by Hype Williams, filming for the video spanned three days and cost approximately $700,000, the largest budget Wallace had had for a video yet. Just over five minutes long, the video plays like a movie, with Wallace and Combs chased by police, both on land and on sea. Other scenes—including one with Wallace and Combs driving backward in a tunnel as well as another involving a black leopard—leaned toward the dizzying excess for which Bad Boy was constantly criticized. But in this case, neither Combs nor Wallace cared. They were going for the gold.

But the police chases depicted on the video weren't altogether unrealistic. While out in Los Angeles, Wallace soon realized federal authorities were actively trailing him. In one particular scene later described by Lil' Cease, the two men were standing outside Wallace's hotel when a car stopped, and a man got out, snapping a picture of Wallace before jumping back in his car and driving away. Cease asked Wallace if he was used to the paparazzi yet. Wallace laughed before responding that the man was a member of the federal authorities and that even if he hated being followed, he knew that at least someone had his back out there.

FINDING RELIGION

While in Los Angeles, Wallace also got his first—and his last—tattoo, the text of the Psalm 27 written on faded parchment paper. It read:

The Lord is my light and my salvation, whom shall I fear?
The Lord is the truth of my life, of whom shall I be afraid?
When the wicked, even my enemies and foes, came upon me to
     bite my flesh
They stumbled and fell.

Wallace mentioned God several times in a few different interviews, even telling a reporter, "A lot of...[men] want to give up and do wrong, but they don't even think God is in their corner" (Coker, 2003, p. 236). There seemed to be little reason for the sudden appearance of religious tones in his life. Although he never claimed to have found religion, he did replace his usual gold Bad Boy pendant with a massive gold and diamond cross and talked some about religion in his last interview, noting the role he felt God could take in his life.

THE SOUL TRAIN AWARDS

Again wanting to work the Los Angeles crowd, Wallace attended the Soul Train Awards in March 1996, not just as an artist but also as a presenter, slated to give singer Toni Braxton her award for best R&B/soul album for her latest release, *Secrets*. The annual event was held in Los Angeles's Shrine Auditorium, a historic landmark that played host to many of entertainment's largest events. That night, Wallace was dressed to the nines, and per usual, Combs was right along with him, as were Cease and the R&B group 112, who had recently signed to Bad Boy. There was little representation of Death Row at the ceremony, given that their most noted rapper—Tupac Shakur—was now dead, and their president was imprisoned.

But as Wallace's name was called, and he walked down the carpeted aisle toward the stage, a booing erupted in the balcony seats, a spot open to the general public. Once on stage, Wallace looked toward were the jeers were loudest and asked, "What up, Cali?" The boos became louder, and Wallace simply smiled. They soon stopped, and Wallace presented the award as planned.

But even with the brave front, Wallace was disturbed, a topic he discussed even after the Bad Boy camp had returned to the hotel. But his reflection couldn't last long. Studio time was booked, and Wallace was supposed to add his part to "It's All about the Benjamins." He was also supposed to fly out to London in the morning for more promotion of his upcoming album, though he was already planning to skip the flight. While in his hotel room, Wallace conducted what was to be his last interview. While watching a recast of the awards on television, Wallace answered questions about his children, the way his life had turned out, and where he feels it was going. He talked candidly about Evans, Lil' Kim, and the relationships he had that he felt were no longer positive. He said that he was no longer viewing life as an everyday struggle, but instead was looking at it as an opportunity, and that he still had so much to give.

After the interview, he and some friends went to see the movie *Donnie Brasco*, a police drama in which Johnny Depp plays a police officer who infiltrates the mob, only to find his pretend life taking over his real life. Right after the movie, Wallace went to the studio and recorded several tracks for Combs's new album, incorporating the movie into his rhymes. As soon as he was finished recording, Wallace went home, ready to sleep. He knew the next day would be long.

Chapter 7

DEATH IN LOS ANGELES

Originally scheduled to fly to London on a promotional tour early on March 8, Wallace opted to instead stay in Los Angeles, where he and Combs had spent the last four months at the Westwood Marquis. Later in the day, while on the phone with his mother in what would prove to be their last conversation, he explained that he could do interviews about his upcoming album over the phone instead of in person, freeing up time to work more on Combs's debut album, then called *Hell Up in Harlem*. He also planned to do more West Coast promotion for his upcoming album *Life after Death*, which was scheduled to hit the streets March 25. He would soon tape the video for the album's first single, "Hypnotize," which was already showing up on mix tapes across the country after receiving heavy play on national radio. Because of the bicoastal tension between the Death Row and Bad Boy camps, Wallace felt it important to garner as much support as he could on the left coast, an attempt he felt would help narrow the gap between the two rap capitals, Los Angeles and New York City.

But even though work kept him in Los Angeles, Wallace was also a bit worried about security in London, he told his mother. He thought that not enough guards were hired and that the trip wasn't well planned. In Los Angeles, he relied on off-duty police to provide much-needed security. In London, he wouldn't have that luxury. Wallace was always worried about security, something that had become a common topic after Shakur was gunned down in Vegas. Wallace told *Los Angeles Times* reporter Cheo Hodari Coker just a month shy of his own death how Tupac Shakur wasn't properly protected, leading to his death:

[Rappers] making so much money, their lifestyle should be more protected.... Their lives should be more protected where things like a drive-by shooting ain't supposed to happen. That shouldn't have happened, man. He's supposed to have lots of security. He ain't even supposed to be sitting next to no window. (Coker, 2003, p. 5)

Wallace told his mother he felt safe and comfortable on the West Coast, despite having moved hotels at least five times during his month-long stay, moves that resulted largely from security concerns. He even looked at several vacation homes in the area and told several friends and family he thought this was a place he could spend his leisure time. He was comfortable there, Voletta Wallace would later tell a reporter. "Maybe he felt too comfortable," she said (Scott, 2001, p. 6).

She later said he also talked about presenting at the Soul Train Awards and the way the crowd responded to him, about how the boos still rang in his head. He expressed this same thought to longtime friend Lance "Un" Rivera, whom he called after talking to his mother. He told Rivera that the world would change on March 25 when *Life after Death* was released and that he would be known as the "nicest M.C." (Scott, 2001, p. 2). He told Rivera he felt sure this album would a turning point for rap. Not only had he carried his trademark narrative style farther in this album than he had before, but he had also employed more storylines, placing himself as the center of a mafia-style family, complete with grandiose descriptions of money, possessions, and women, subjects common in the burgeoning mafioso style of rap.

The night before, he expressed similar thoughts to old girlfriend Jan Jackson, T'Yanna's mother. On the phone, he was relaxed, she said. They laughed like they hadn't in years and talked for more than an hour, like old friends. He told her his high expectations for the album, as well as his concerns over security, claiming that with Death Row's Marion "Suge" Knight behind bars, many of the problems they'd encountered with the West Coast would continue to dissipate. High-profile rappers like Snoop were showcasing East Coast performers. New York rappers like Wallace were also attempting to embrace the West Coast, and Wallace even included a song on his upcoming *Life after Death* called "Goin' Back to Cali": "If I got to choose a coast, I got to choose the East," but Wallace rapped, that didn't mean he couldn't spend time on the West Coast. On the phone, Wallace told Jackson he planned to spend the evening working on Combs's album and recovering from the sting of the crowd's reaction the night before at the awards. He mentioned a party downtown, though he didn't seem enthusiastic, she said. Hosted by *Vibe* magazine and Qwest Records, Quincy Jones's label, the party was being held at the Peterson Automotive Museum on the corner of Fairfax and Wilshire in downtown Los Angeles and was considered the official after-party of the awards, despite being held a day later. But Wallace said that he doubted he'd go, that he was ready to just relax.

But after some persuasion from Combs, Wallace agreed to attend. It would be a good opportunity to show the West Coast he hadn't been stopped by their reaction the night before, Combs later said Wallace told him. He didn't want to go to the studio. He was like, 'I finished my album. I just want to celebrate with you. I just want to have a good time. Let's go to this *Vibe* joint. Hopefully I can meet some people, let them know I want to do some acting.' That made me proud; he was thinking like a businessman," Combs told a reporter (Gilmore, 1997).

CATCHING A VIBE

Meeting first at Motown Records head Andre Harrell's house, the Bad Boy group headed downtown. Shortly after 9 P.M., Wallace, Combs, Lil' Cease, James Lloyd, and Damien "D-Roc" Butler arrived at the museum, headed for the second floor. Wallace was dressed in faded blue jeans and a long-sleeved, button-up black velour shirt, with a large, solid-gold Jesus pendant around his neck. By his side was his walking cane, a standard accompaniment since his car accident the previous September. On his head was his trademark riding cap that, like always, matched his outfit. He wasn't dressed in the persona of the Notorious B.I.G., or even of Biggie Smalls. Instead, he was just Christopher, friends later said.

Wallace, along with the rest of the Bad Boy camp, knew this night was theirs, and despite the chilly reception the evening before, almost everyone in attendance was a friend or at least respected the group. Once the men were inside, the respect flowed, with celebrities eager to say hello and the women always close by. Wallace and Combs made their way to a corner booth, where they sat as women danced for Wallace, tossing smiles his way as he sat watching, talking to the others at his table. Many at the party later discussed how relaxed he looked, almost more so then than in recent times.

Like most industry parties, this one was packed with various artists, celebrities, producers, music executives, and other entertainment professionals, including Wallace's estranged wife, Faith Evans; Marion "Suge" Knight's wife, Sharitha Knight; Heavy D; Jermaine Dupri; Busta Rhymes; Kidada Jones; Def Jam founder Russell Simmons; actors Chris

Tucker and Wesley Snipes; and singer Whitney Houston. Nearly 2,000 people were at the party, including various Bloods and Crips, among them, Orlando Anderson and his uncle, Dwayne "Keefee D" Davis, two of the men implicated in Shakur's shooting and both members of the Southside Crips. DJ Quik arrived with about a dozen members of the Treetop Piru Bloods. But despite the gang presence, no one at the party noted any sort of the drama that usually happens when opposing gangs are gathered in the same room. Instead, the atmosphere was light and happy, with bottles of Cristal constantly popped as blunts were continually rolled. On the stereo, Wallace's single "Hypnotize" loudly played eight times in a row. The dance floor was crowded with women who let up a cheer each time the song was replayed. Wallace was the star of the night.

"I was throwing paper at him, telling him how much I liked his record," Def Jam founder Russell Simmons told Coker (Coker, 2003, p. 241). "These girls were dancing for him, and he was just sittin' there, not even moving his cane. I wanted to be like him. He was so cool, so funny and calm."

THE END OF THE PARTY

Because the lobby downstairs was packed with people, and the main ballroom was at almost double its capacity, fire marshals were called just after midnight, and they quickly decided to shut down the party. It wasn't the end of the night, though. Interscope executive Steven Stoute had already planned to host a private after-party at his house. On the way out, Wallace and Combs stopped to take a photo. Neither smiled as they stared straight into the camera, their expressions serious. This would be the last photo Wallace ever took. The pair took their time leaving the museum because Wallace's leg still hurt, making steps a bit difficult.

Outside, fans crowded the exit, yelling names as the occasional camera flashed. At about 12:40, Wallace, Combs, and the others left the museum, stopping at the valet stand to chat with friends about Stoute's party. Headed toward their cars—which were parked on the street less than a block away—Wallace turned back to the group, saying, "See y'all at the next party" (Scott, 2001, p. 8).

But when they got to the cars, the men decided to instead just head back to the hotel, taking advantage of an early night to bed so that they would be ready for the studio in the morning. Combs and Wallace got into their separate SUVs. Combs sat shotgun in a white Suburban, with factotum Kenneth Story at the wheel. With him were his usual three bodyguards, in the backseat. Wallace rode in a dark green 1997 GMC Chevy Suburban, his dark skin bright against the white leather seats. On the bumper was a sticker that read "Think B.I.G. March 25, 1997," a promotion for his upcoming album. Bucking his own rules about sitting next to a window, Wallace rode in the passenger seat as Gregory "G-Money" Young climbed behind the wheel. D-Roc and Lil' Cease sat in the back seats. As soon as the car was started, a tape of *Life after Death* began loudly playing from the stereo as fans waved, and Wallace smiled back.

The Bad Boy caravan soon pulled into traffic, with Combs's vehicle in front. Behind him was a Ford Blazer filled with off-duty police officers from the Inglewood Police Department—the same group often employed by Death Row's Suge Knight—who there as bodyguards for Combs and Wallace. The light at the intersection of Wilshire and Fairfax, less than three hundred feet from the museum, turned yellow, and Combs's car cruised through. Young pulled the Suburban to a stop, and almost as if from nowhere, a white Toyota Land Cruiser came from the opposite way, making a U-turn in the middle of the street in an attempt to cut off the Ford Blazer. Almost as quickly, a dark-colored Chevy Impala pulled alongside the passenger side of Wallace's Suburban. In the driver's seat was a well-dressed black man who appeared to be in his early thirties and who had a fade haircut. He wore a dark-colored suit—along with a bow tie—his outfit resembling the kind often worn by members of the Nation of Islam. Later, witnesses would say he turned to Wallace and rolled down his window, his left hand still on the wheel. With his right he pulled out a blue steel 9-millimeter semiautomatic and opened fire.

Shots rang out into the night as everyone on the street—and inside the Suburban—ducked for cover. Only Wallace remained still, his bulking figure jerking slightly as four slugs tore through the door of the Suburban, cutting through his chest and abdomen.

People in the crowd screamed as the Impala drove away. Lil' Cease lifted his head just in time to get a glimpse of the guy before the car left. Soon Butler and G-Money lifted their heads as well—and within seconds realized that Wallace wasn't moving.

"Biggie ducked and stayed all the way down," D-Roc Butler later told the *Los Angeles Times* in an interview. "If he had made it, I could see by the look on his face that he could tell you who the shooter was. But he didn't have time to say a word. He didn't say, 'Ouch.' He didn't say, 'Yo, look out.' He didn't say nothin'" (Philips, 2006).

Having stopped his SUV just after passing through the intersection, Combs jumped out of his car and ran over to Wallace, who was still hunched over. From the crowd came the others who knew Wallace—including Wallace's manager, Mark Pitts, and Faith Evans, both of whom were still outside the museum—as Combs, Damian, and Lil' Cease tried to pull Wallace from the car. But with Wallace weighing a heavy 390 pounds, they could barely budge the unconscious rapper and were able only to sit him back in his seat, closing the passenger door. Once he was leaned back, they realized Wallace's eyes were open, though staring blankly, and his tongue hung limply out the corner of his mouth. Combs stepped into the car, sitting behind Wallace, as Story pushed Young aside and took the wheel.

A hospital—Cedars-Sinai Medical Center—was only 15 blocks away, and instead of waiting for an ambulance to respond, Story slammed down the gas pedal, honking his horn as he pulled into traffic. With the Suburban as their ambulance, Story slid through intersections, running red lights as he made his way through to the hospital.

Pulling up to the emergency rooms, Damian jumped from the SUV, running into the emergency room as he yelled for help. Technicians immediately came to the car and, on seeing Wallace's generous size, called for more help. Less than a minute later, six technicians pulled Wallace out, laying him on a stretcher. Combs ran alongside the gurney, through the crowded emergency room, stopping just short of the double doors that led to the trauma center and surgical rooms.

Shocked, Combs waited inside the lobby of the ER. Combs got down on his knees, quietly praying, as Lil' Cease lay on the hospital linoleum, his head in his hands, his sobs loud in the busy ER. Soon others joined, including Evans, who got to the hospital almost as quickly as Wallace himself. Even more people stood outside the emergency rooms, hands clasped in a group prayer, many crying. The press had already arrived, along with police, who taped off the Suburban.

Back inside the surgery rooms, doctors realized Wallace had extensive internal bleeding, with irreparable damage to several organs. He never regained consciousness. Doctors tried to resuscitate him for nearly 20 minutes but to no avail. At 1:15 A.M. on March 9, Christopher George Latore Wallace was declared dead. He was only 24.

He was killed just a few days shy of the six-month anniversary of Tupac Shakur's murder, which was then—as now—still unsolved, as Wallace's would remain. With this second celebrity hip-hop shooting in less than six months, the genre of music seemed to be living up to its violent lyrics, a violence that would only worsen as theories surrounding Wallace's death arose.

Within minutes of his death, after a surgeon told a destitute Combs and Evans they had been unable to save Wallace, news quickly began to spread. Newspapers—and especially the *Los Angeles Times*—set to the difficult task of separating fact from fiction, taking eyewitness reports and checking with various unnamed sources on possible triggermen.

Two of the nation's largest urban radio stations—Los Angeles's Power 106 and New York City's Hot 97—aired a national simulcast playing Wallace's songs, encouraging fans and artists to call in with any thoughts on Wallace's death. Among them was Dr. Dre, who said, "We need to talk intelligently and tell people there is no rivalry [between the East Coast and West Coast]." An emotional Q-Tip from A Tribe Called Quest also called, saying, "We need to wake up. If we say we're ready to die, we're going to die" (Philips, 1997).

Anticipating high album sales, record stores placed calls to distributor Atlantic Records for more albums to pack their shelves. Vendors began making shirts that would bear his likeness along with the dates of his birth and now death. And, almost as quickly as he was killed, theories about his gunman began to swarm.

THEORIES ON HIS DEATH

For many, the murder was just further proof of the war between the East and West coasts, placing Death Row Records head Suge Knight as the proverbial triggerman. Some claimed it was retaliation for the murder of Knight's friend Jason Robeles just two years earlier in Atlanta. Some thought Knight ordered a hit that was meant for Combs, not Wallace. Still others thought that it was a simple defense of territory and a matter of jealousy of their success, and that despite Knight's being in jail, he still resented Bad Boy's presence in Los Angeles. Some still believed he was responsible for Shakur's death, choosing to have the popular rapper killed instead of letting him step away from the label, as Shakur had planned to do.

There were striking similarities between the murders of Wallace and Shakur. Both were the only ones hit, despite sitting close to their drivers and, in Wallace's case, a full entourage. Both were without their usual bodyguards, and both relied on off-duty LAPD officers for protection, officers later found to be closely connected to Death Row Records (*Frontline*, 2001). Orlando Anderson was at the scene of both murders, and his uncle "Keefe D" had access to cars similar to those used in the murders. Both men were murdered in front of hundreds of people, but few witnesses stepped forward, including their label managers, who were there at the time of the shootings. Police believed these coincidences to be too convenient and immediately looked to Knight as a primary suspect.

"It's ludicrous for anyone to blame Death Row. Snoop and Biggie and Puffy have been in the press recently trying to squash all the media madness," Norris Anderson told *Los Angeles Times* reporter Chuck Philips hours after Wallace's death. Anderson ran Death Row while Knight was imprisoned. "This is a terrible tragedy. Death Row knows how bad something like this can feel. It happened in our own backyard with Tupac just a few months ago. My condolences go out to Biggie's family. I feel horrible for them. This killing has got to stop" (Philips, 1997).

Regardless, Knight was largely considered a suspect from the beginning, a sentiment expressed in many of the stories that were soon to follow, including the one published in the *Los Angeles Times* just a few hours after Wallace's death. Others believed a crazed fan who blamed Wallace for Shakur's death pulled the trigger, and even more blamed local gangs for the death. Some claimed that Combs had hired Crips to provide security for Wallace while they were in Los Angeles a year earlier and that Combs had never paid his tab. Combs has always vehemently denied hiring Crips or owing any gang money.

"We've never hired Crips or any other gang members to do security for us," Combs later told MTV News reporter Kurt Loder, shortly after Wallace's murder. "But the misconception is that because we're young and black, we're not handling business like anybody else."

But LAPD authorities—and especially detective Russell Poole, who would later take over the case—knew from informants about Combs's interaction with gangs, and he dismissed Combs's claims of never employing gang members for security. It was reported that at the 1996 Soul Train Awards, just one year earlier, Combs had openly employed gang members, who attended the show alongside the Bad Boy camp. The day before Wallace's death, sources placed both Combs and Wallace at a basketball game at Cal State Dominguez Hills, and informants later told police that they stopped afterward at the nearby Crips headquarters, where they spent a good deal of time (Sullivan, 2005). According to several sources, Combs denied any interaction with gang members, a stance he has maintained since the ties were first alleged. Immediately following Wallace's death, and once back in New York City, Combs would meet with police only at his attorney's office.

There were other complications to the case. Despite the case clearly being a murder, the immediate investigation did not include any detectives from the LAPD's Robbery-Homicide Division, although they were aware of the details of Wallace's death.

"They were there that first night," a former LAPD lieutenant told author Randall Sullivan. "But they were gone by the next morning and didn't come back to the case until an entire month had passed. In thirty years, I had never seen that: a murder case involving a major celebrity that wasn't taken over by Robbery-Homicide right out of the gate" (Sullivan, 2003, p. 123).

This was just one of the many failings of the LAPD in covering the case, failings that later resulted in the largest police scandal in LAPD history. Despite hundreds of witnesses and a composite drawing of the shooter, the police department seemed to have few leads and no suspects, even when given names by informants. Instead, the shooting was treated as no more than a gang hit, despite evidence to the contrary.

It was also revealed soon after Wallace's death that approximately a dozen police officers were on the scene when Wallace was shot, and at least a half dozen officers were working as security for the rapper. In addition, an array of undercover officers from the Federal Bureau of Alcohol, Tobacco and Firearms as well as the New York Police Department were trailing Wallace. New York police believed the assailant who had shot Shakur had also killed an off-duty police officer and was working for Combs in Los Angeles. ATF officers were investigating claims that Death Row employees were selling stolen weapons, laundering money, and selling massive amounts of cocaine. Investigating officers—and Detective Poole most of all—later told reporter Randall Sullivan there was not a solid reason why none of these officers or authorities were able to catch a glimpse of the gunman, which some believed indicated the involvement between the police and Death Row (Sullivan, 2005).

GOING HOME

Wallace's mother, Voletta Wallace, boarded a plane for Los Angeles, arriving on March 10 to see a barrage of television coverage on the LAX terminal televisions. From there she went to her son's hotel, making her way through the thick crowd gathered outside and finding quiet inside his room, where she stayed alone for some time before heading to Evans's hotel, where her grandson waited.

But even as theories on Wallace's death multiplied, for Voletta Wallace, Jan Jackson, and Faith Evans, reality set in as the three identified his body in the Los Angeles County Morgue. Soon plans for his funeral were made, with industry icon and Arista Records executive Clive Davis handling most of the arrangements, and within just a few days, Wallace's body was returned to New York, his last trip home. He was on the same flight as his mother. "I thought about the trips that Christopher and I had taken to Jamaica every summer since he was a little boy," she wrote in her book *Biggie: Voletta Wallace Remembers Her Son, Christopher Wallace,*

AKA Notorious B.I.G. "Those were good thoughts because they took me away from the heart-wrenching thought of him lying in the belly of the airplane. I kept thinking of him underneath me and it was ripping my heart to pieces....My cargo was my son" (Wallace and McKenzie, 2005, p. 125).

As authorities had loaded Wallace's body onto a plane, candles and flowers still adorned the front of the Peterson Automobile Museum, and in Brooklyn, similar vigils were held outside his childhood home in Brooklyn, at the Brownstone he and his mother had shared at 226 St. James, his old stoop now filled with cards, stuffed animals, flowers, candles, and pictures. Stores swelled with copies of *Ready to Die* as street vendors hawked t-shirts bearing his image as well as the dates May 21, 1972–March 9, 1997. Near his house, locals painted graffiti on empty walls, all a homage to their hometown hero.

Davis had selected the funeral home that would receive Wallace's body, the Frank E. Campbell Funeral Home, one of the few places equipped to handle the services for a famous person. There they prepared Wallace for his last appearance, dressing him in a white, double-breasted suit typical of the Mafioso style Wallace had adopted as his fame grew, a choice made by his manager.

On March 19, the crowds gathered outside that fancy Upper West Side funeral home as the private service began inside, a formal affair that required doormen checking identification even of the most famous rap stars. In attendance were Evans and Voletta Wallace, who rode to the service together, as well as Combs, Lil' Kim, Lil' Cease, and the rest of Wallace's friends. Other hip-hop heavies, including Mary J. Blige, Dr. Dre, Public Enemy, Queen Latifah, Flavor Flav, Busta Rhymes, Heavy D, and Jay-Z, were there as well. Only 350 people were allowed to attend the service, which included a eulogy delivered by Combs, several verses from the Book of Job read by Voletta Wallace, and a deliverance of "Walk With Me, Jesus" by Faith Evans that reportedly brought most in attendance to tears.

THE BLACK HEART PROCESSION

Pallbearers Damien "D-Roc" Butler, Lance "Un" Rivera, and Lamont "Lil' Cease" Mosley carried Wallace's heavy casket to the shiny black hearse that was to bring his body to its final destination, the Fresh Ponds Crematory in Middle Village, Queens, where he was to be cremated. The hearse headed the procession of eight limos and about 20 cars, including two that were flowered. One spelled B.I.G. in red carnations; another spelled "For Daddy" in yellow.

As is Brooklyn tradition, the procession traveled through his old neighborhood one final time. Already the streets were filled with hundreds of spectators, all crowding the sidewalks on the cold March day, some sitting atop cars while others leaned outside windows and perched on fire escapes. Cops waited in riot gear, as the crowd grew anxious, many having waited outside since early morning. Some were visibly angry at the police presence, and those who lived in the neighborhood and did not want to witness Wallace's last ride shouted angrily at those gathered, sparking small fights that almost always subsided as quickly as they began. Many cried as the procession passed them.

And finally, the procession entered Wallace's neighborhood, and at the helm was a man on a bicycle carrying a hand-printed sign that read, "Christopher Wallace, The Greatest of All Time." The procession slowly snaked through the Brooklyn streets as the crowd cheered, the family and friends inside the cars waving to the gathered fans. But nearly as quickly as it began, the procession ended, the last car leaving the neighborhood less than 10 minutes from when it first arrived.

Almost instantly, the song "Hypnotize" played loudly on a boom box on Fulton Street, and with the first beats came a discernable change in the crowd, a certain rowdiness that settled in as some danced atop cars, on dumpsters, and in the streets. The cops soon began arresting random people, though they were unable to contain the crowd. Soon a SWAT team arrived, bringing with them more riot police, and armed with their Plexiglas shields and nightsticks, they violently weaved through the crowd, arresting some and knocking back others. Cameras flashed as the cops futilely tried to disperse the crowd using all their means, including pepper spray, which was sprayed into the eyes of *New York Times* stringer Julia Campbell, a young woman who was sprayed after showing her press pass. In less than 20 minutes, the crowd was gone, with only a few remaining as "Hypnotize" played in loop.

Chapter 8

LIFE AFTER DEATH

Both the title and the cover art belie the songs within Notorious B.I.G.'s accidental epilogue *Life after Death*, a lengthy exposition into his world of constant struggle and survival set against a mafioso background. With Wallace positioned against a hearse, the album cover itself proves a metaphor for what was to happen just days before the album was released, an album whose title was also a fitting tribute to the man whose name and style still endure more than a decade later.

A double-disc recording, *Life After Death* features a staff and process unlike many albums released at the time. Many of its beats were recorded in mid-1996 at a Trinidad recording studio, where Combs took his "Hit-men," an elite team of producers and engineers, to work on the album in what has been described as an assembly line. There the rawness that first attracted listeners to Wallace in *Ready to Die* was smoothed into something akin to a big-budget movie, a sound that was as polished and professional as the rapper now aimed to be.

Wallace recorded his tracks at Daddy's House, Combs's new studio, after producers assembled the beats and after his devastating accident that left his femur shattered. Before, on *Ready to Die*, Easy Mo Bee, the RZA, and others had worked alongside Wallace as the songs were developed. Now, the music waited for him to arrive, the bigger team of producers having spent months developing an album they considered as cohesive as they did smooth, one that was sample-heavy and cleaner, all the while ready for the radio.

At the studio, Wallace and the others were treated to first-class sessions, complete with food trays and private lounges, a far cry from the stripped-down sessions at the Scarsdale home studio where most of *Ready to Die* was recorded. At Daddy's House, his liquor of choice awaited him each day, as did weed and his friends. When Wallace would arrive—usually in the late afternoon or early evening—and would listen to the beats as loud as he could, while Deric "D-Dot" Angelettie, Bad Boy's A&R representative, made sure that everything was organized and on-schedule and that everyone, especially Wallace, was happy.

Released just five days after Wallace's funeral, *Life after Death* remains one of the best-selling rap albums of all time, having sold a formidable 500,000 copies in the first week alone. The album also signaled Wallace's shift from the more realistic depiction of his life found in *Ready to Die* to the mafioso style portrayal of life as a crime lord. Mafioso tends towards self-indulgent rhymes steeped with gangster references, such as to notorious real crime families, as well as characters in movies, such as *Scarface*, *The Streets of New York*, and *Casino*, as proved in the lyrics to "You're Nobody Til Somebody Kills You":

Watch Casino, I'm the hip-hop version of Nicky Tarantino Ask Nino, he know.

A style brought from the underground by Raekwon's *Only Built 4 Cuban Linx*, mafioso saw its first mainstream light with Jay-Z's *Reasonable Doubt* and Nas's mafioso-infused *It Was Written*, released nearly a year before *Life after Death* hit streets.

The album features a strong roster of music heavies, including Jay-Z, Mase, Carl Thomas, Faith Evans, Too $hort, and R. Kelly. Running nearly two hours, the album is cleaner and more radio-ready than *Ready to Die*, with singles such as "Hypnotize," "Mo Money, Mo Problems," and "Sky's the Limit" primed for radio play. The first two of those singles peaked at no. 1 on the Billboard Hot 100, as well as landing at top positions on both the Billboard Hot R&B/Hip-Hop and Hot Rap Tracks. "Sky's the Limit" didn't fare as well, landing on only the Canadian charts. The album itself hit no. 1 on the charts.

Often considered one of the best hip-hop albums, many publications list *Life after Death* in its top lists, including *Rolling Stone*, *Blender*, *Vibe*, and *The Source*. It samples many songs, including ones by Schoolly D, Diana Ross, Herb Alpert, and Public Enemy. For many, though, the album falls short of the promise offered by *Ready to Die*, a weakness largely attributed to Combs, who used this album as one of his more comprehensive offerings as executive producer, often weighing heavily in on its songs, his pop style heavy beneath Wallace's lyrics.

In the lyrics of the album are various references to inevitable death, an end that comes regardless of wealth or fame, as evidenced in the lyrics from "You're Nobody Til Somebody Kills You":

> You can be the shit, flash the fattest five . . . but when your shell get hit
> You ain't worth spit, just a memory

Life after Death stands in stark contrast to his first album, both in theme and in style. Jay-Z once said that *Ready to Die* was like the work of an outsider looking in, of a man angry at his life as a dealer and soon to be a father, of someone who worked for each scrap of food he ate. By contrast, *Life after Death* portrayed someone on the inside looking out, showing how all that glitters isn't gold and how death is always knocking at his front door.

The video for the album's first single, "Hypnotize," turned out to be the last Wallace would ever film. Directed by Hype Williams, the second video for the album—"Mo Money, Mo Problems"—starred Combs, then performing as Puff Daddy, and Mase, both of whom wore sparkling track suits, ushering in what would later be called hip-hop's "Shiny Suit" phase, which largely coincided with the onset of hip-hop bling.

Both "Hypnotize" and "Mo Money, Mo Problems" hit no. 1 on the Billboard Hot 100, a posthumous success that Wallace was the first to achieve. The album's third single, "Sky's the Limit," didn't fare as well, though its video was popular. Directed by Spike Jonze, the video features children portraying Wallace, Combs, Evans, and the others in what many considered a clever alternative to either only using older footage of Wallace or not representing him at all. In a Sesame Street version of what had become a typical Bad Boy video, the children pose around a pool as girls dance; appear behind the wheel of a Mercedes driving down a tunnel, arriving amid throngs of fan at the club; and dance in a darkened room while talking to the camera. Per Bad Boy fashion, the entire video showcases extravagant wealth, with the children dressed to the nines in their Sunday finest.

A few months after Wallace's death, Combs brought in Faith Evans and R&B quartet 112 to record a tribute to Wallace. Written by rapper Sauce Money, the song heavily samples from the Police hit single "Every Breath You Take," also borrowing some from the hymn "I'll Fly Away," playing into the song's theme that Wallace was in heaven, or at least some place after his death. The song features Combs rapping, with Evans weighing in on the chorus, as does 112. The song debuted at no. 1 on the Billboard Hot 100, one of the few rappers to ever do so. Sauce Money later won a Grammy for the song.

OTHER RELEASES

Since Wallace's death, Bad Boy has released three Notorious B.I.G. albums: *Born Again, Duets: The Final Chapter,* and *Greatest Hits.* All debuted to high sales, high rankings, and strong criticism, with many fans and music journalists feeling the albums represented a common complaint about Bad Boy and Sean Combs: he's just in it for the money. Both *Duets* and *Born Again* heavily—and sometimes eerily—rehash old material, given that almost everything Wallace had recorded by the time of his death had already found its way onto records, leaving few unreleased tracks, and those that did remain were found in *Born Again.*

Released in December 1999, *Born Again* debuted to lackluster reviews by critics and a lukewarm reception by fans, something many attribute to its fragmented nature. Using old and unreleased lyrics and outtakes from his earlier studio efforts, *Born Again* lacks Wallace's usual charm and flavor, instead heavily relying on guest appearances from industry heavyweights, such as Eminem, Snoop Doggy Dogg, Busta Rhymes, Redman, Mobb Depp, Missy Elliott, and Nas, as well as the usual collaborators, Lil' Kim, Combs, and Junior M.A.F.I.A. The album, largely produced by DJ Premier and Deric "D-Dot" Angelettie, featured new beats beneath old lyrics, resulting in an album that is largely forgettable save one track, "Dead Wrong," which features Wallace at his finest, with lyrics well-complemented by Eminem.

Much of the criticism that followed this album was similar to the criticism of the later release, *Duets: The Final Chapter,* whose manufactured collaborations many hardcore fans resented. For instance, one song pits Wallace with the long-dead Bob Marley. Another has him with rock group Korn. The album also coincided with "B.I.G. Mobile Month," which was a promotion offering up ringtone versions of Wallace's songs.

"I think it's very sad and very painful to see them constantly pushing out these rehashed albums because the bottom line is that they don't exactly enhance Biggie's legacy," said *New Nation* music editor Justin Onyeka. "It's obviously a money-making thing, a great money-making opportunity for Puffy and Bad Boy" (Egere-Cooper, 2006).

And although Voletta Wallace agrees that there is money to be made, she maintains the album was for his fans. "Everybody that's on this album makes money," Voletta Wallace told reporter Matilda Egere-Cooper about the *Duets* album. "The artists make money, we make money. But this album was made for Christopher's children, yes and for me, and for Faith. And not only that, but to give the audience something of my son, something that they asked for, and something that they really needed" (Egere-Cooper, 2006).

Released almost 10 years to the day after Wallace was killed, Bad Boy Records' release of *The Greatest Hits* did not come without criticism. Though *Duets* was somewhat well received at the time, *Greatest Hits* was largely considered by many as another effort by Combs—and even Voletta Wallace and Faith Evans—to make more money in the name of Bad Boy's flagship artist.

As a *Rolling Stone* reviewer pointed out, "If you were already into Wallace, you already had the albums from which these songs were pulled." Still, though, the album enjoyed high sales, demonstrating that even if the songs aren't new, they are still good, and in the 10 years between his death and the *Greatest Hits'* release, many new hip-hop fans were born, some of whom possibly never owned a Notorious B.I.G. album.

But though Bad Boy has come under considerable fire for the releases, Wallace's family and label aren't the first to cash in on post-death sales. Many musicians have found posthumous success, from classical composer Chopin to indie rocker Elliot Smith. Without a doubt, Elvis Presley continues to be one of the best-selling artists in history, though there were few posthumous albums that actually gave listeners new material. The same could be said for Bob Marley, with his posthumous albums largely containing already-released songs.

Otis Redding's hit "(Sittin' on) the Dock of the Bay" was recorded just three days before his death in December 1967. It was released the following month and was an instant no. 1 hit that sold millions. His album *Hard to Handle* was released in 1968 and was successful, though not as much as the single "(Sittin' on) the Dock of the Bay." Other records were released, including *History of Otis Redding* (1968), *The Immortal Otis Redding* (1968), *Love Man* (1969), and *Tell the Truth* (1970), among several others. Approximately 17 singles have been released posthumously, and most have fared well on the Billboard charts.

Redding received the Grammy Lifetime Achievement Award in 1999. Three years later, his hometown of Macon honored the musician with a memorial statue in the city's Gateway Park. He is still consistently ranked among the top artists of all time, often placing high. His music has been sampled by several artists, including Kanye West, who used parts of his song "It's Too Late" in his song "Gone."

Eazy-E's *Str8 Off the Muthaphukkin Streets of Compton* contained 14 previously unreleased tracks, all recorded the year before Eazy died from complications related to AIDS. Although the original plan was for a two-disc album, Eazy was unable to finish the rest of the album before his death. The album—which was his second full-length album—debuted to lackluster sales in late November 1995. It featured two singles—"Just Tah Let U Know" and "Muthaphukkin Real"—but neither placed on the Billboard charts.

Few artists have reached the posthumous success of Tupac Shakur, who had dozens of unreleased songs recorded at the time of his death in September 1996. One of his most famous posthumous albums, *The Don Killuminati—The 7-Day Theory*, is considered one of the most iconic albums of all times, and one of his more recent albums, 2004's *Loyal to the Game*, reached no. 1 on the Billboard album charts within a week of its release, having sold approximately 330,000 copies within days. It marked Shakur's fifth no. 1 full-length album and was the third to hit that mark since his death. According to Nielson SoundScan, Shakur has sold 24 million albums, with about 18 million of those sales coming after his death. He still remains the best-selling rapper of all time, an achievement he is not likely to lose anytime soon, given that almost every new album released debuts at the top of the charts, where it continually racks up high sales and positive reviews. He is a standard on "best-of" lists and is one of the most cited influential rappers.

The main difference between Shakur's and Wallace's posthumous releases lies with Shakur's abundance of unreleased material; he recorded several songs a day for several weeks immediately following his arrest. One of rap's most prolific artists, Shakur still reportedly has unreleased tracks, though their future remains as uncertain as that of the label Death Row, which still owns all the masters.

WHO SHOT YA

As Wallace's funeral procession snaked through the streets of Brooklyn, in California a car chase erupted on a Los Angeles street, at the intersection of Lankershim and Ventura. A green, decked-out Mitsubishi Montero pulled up beside an older, beat Buick Regal. The driver of the Montero was a well-dressed and well-groomed black man flossing his teeth; the driver of the Regal, an older white man, his salt and pepper hair long and shaggy beneath his black cap that proudly displayed a marijuana leaf, a mismatched accessory to his stained wifebeater. According to reports that were later filed, the black man was staring the white man down, and one soon asked the other if there was a problem, which led to an argument that quickly became a chase once the light changed. Within just a few blocks, the white man, LAPD officer Frank Lyga, desperately called for backup, his request growing more frantic as soon as he saw the black man pull a gun, taking aim at Lyga. But Lyga moved first, neatly placing two bullets in his head, the Montero crashing as the driver died.

On the scene, officers quickly recognized the driver of the Mitsubishi as Kevin Gaines, another officer on the LAPD force, assigned to the force's Pacific Division. Gaines was a man known for his quick temper and unwarranted car chases, having been reprimanded for two already that year. A quick check revealed a startling fact: the car wasn't registered to Gaines but instead to Death Row Records. Receipts inside Gaines's wallet revealed he had paid nearly $1,000 for a single lunch just a few days earlier at Monty's, a popular Death Row hangout. There were nine credit cards in his wallet, with each carrying a high limit. Gaines had recently taken to wearing designer clothes, including Versace shirts that reportedly cost more than a grand each. He owned several cars, including a BMW and a Mercedes, possessions that seemed impossible for a man with a family of four making just over $50,000. The tag for the Mitsubishi read "IT-SOKIA," a reference many felt was to internal affairs, the division inside the police department that investigated other officers.

The LAPD soon realized that Gaines had been dating Sharitha Knight, Suge Knight's ex-wife and Snoop Doggy Dogg's former manager. The two reportedly had met at a car wash and had been having an affair for more than a year. Authorities found in his locker pictures of Death Row artists. Unnamed informants alleged that he often acted as a lookout during high-end drug deals, and when his car was searched, a drug dog picked up the faint scent of cocaine.

It all made sense. Less than a year earlier, in August 1996, two LAPD officers had responded to a 9-1-1 call that shots were coming from Sharitha Knight's mansion, with a victim lying near the swimming pool; the caller described a suspect as around 30 years old with a muscular build, not taller than five-feet-ten. Once officers arrived on the scene, a drunk Gains stepped up, knocking one of the two men with his shoulder, while saying he hated cops. He was handcuffed but not apprehended, though a later analysis revealed that Gaines himself had placed the 9-1-1 call and that his description of an intruder matched his own physical build and age. The case was handed over to Internal Affairs, and although he was never charged with a crime, he was dismissed from the department. He promptly hired attorney Milton Grimes, who had become famous after representing Rodney King a few years earlier. The two filed a multimillion-dollar lawsuit against the LAPD and the City of Los Angeles, claiming his "emotional and psychological well-being" had been damaged after the dismissal.

Not long after Wallace's murder, LAPD detective Russell Poole received an anonymous tip that Gaines should be investigated in Wallace's death, a tip that prompted the detective and his partner, Fred Miller, to take over the case. Despite initial claims that the murder was simply a gang hit, Poole thought much of the evidence pointed elsewhere. To start, they knew police walkie-talkies had been used to coordinate the efforts of the black Impala and the white Ford. Poole also knew that Wallace was being tailed not only by federal authorities but also by local police, though neither group had a lead. There were hundreds of witnesses, yet hardly anyone stepped forward with any more than a description of the murderer, whom most every witness described as a light-skinned black man with a neatly-trimmed fade haircut and wide eyes, wearing a blue suit. Finally, Wallace was sitting behind a darkly tinted window, meaning someone had to know exactly where he was in the car in order to kill him. There were no shots other than the ones that entered Wallace's body or were lodged in the front passenger's side door, where Wallace sat.

The theory still persisted about Combs and his involvement with the Crips, a theory perpetuated by a *Los Angeles Times* story that came out more than a year later. The headline read, "Personal Dispute Is Focus of Rap Probe," and the subsequent article dissected Combs's many connections to the Crips. Like the rumors just after Wallace's death, the article claimed Combs had shortchanged a group of Crips that protected the Bad Boy group while they were on the West Coast at the Soul Train Music Awards in March 1996. According to several sources, there were countless pictures of Crips lurking around Bad Boy artists, and it was commonly acknowledged then that the gang was working as security for the group. According to the same sources, and as published in the *Los Angeles Times*, the Crips expected close to $1 million for protecting the artists. Combs allegedly offered only $10,000 and immediately left town. Upon Combs and Wallace's return in 1997, the Crips allegedly asked Combs for the money they felt was owed to them. He refused, and sources say the Crips took their anger out on Wallace.

Combs's association with the Crips first started when both he and Wallace were in Los Angeles promoting *Ready to Die* just after its release. In addition, one of Combs's close friends was Vaughn "Zip" Williams, an older man who often provided security for Bad Boy on the East Coast; Williams was close friends with Dewayne "Keefee D" Davis, Orlando Anderson's uncle. Anderson was the man Knight and the others beat in the lobby of the MGM Grand the night Shakur was killed because he was thought to have stolen a Death Row pendant at a Los Angeles mall, an infraction Knight claimed was punishable by death.

Also, in an article published in *Vibe* magazine, Wrightway Security head Reggie Wright, a former Compton cop and a longtime friend of Knight who often provided security for Knight, pointed the finger at the Compton Crips, claiming Combs's gang connections got Wallace killed. Knight reportedly told police, as well as a few reporters, that Crips were responsible for both deaths, most notably Shakur's, something many found suspicious, given that gang members never ratted each other out, even if they were members of opposite gangs.

On the street, in publications, and at the police station, all signs pointed to Suge Knight. A trusted jailhouse informant imprisoned at California's Corcoran State Prison claimed his cellmate—Marcus Nunn, a Mob Piru Blood and an old associate of Knight's—told him Knight not only hired someone to kill Shakur, but also hired another Mob Piru gang member to murder Wallace. Under the request of anonymity, a Death Row employee claimed to have hard evidence that Knight ordered Wallace's death, though police reportedly never followed up on this information. And with mounting evidence of the police's illegal involvement, as well as the upper brass's reluctance to pursue possible connections between its officers and Wallace's murder, Knight seemed even more at the helm of a rather dirty affair.

OFFICERS' INVOLVEMENT WITH DEATH ROW

LAPD officer Richard McCauley was in Las Vegas the night Shakur was murdered, one of several working as security staff for Death Row. He had officially applied for a permit to work with the label, though that permit was revoked in 1996, months before Shakur's murder. At the time, Mc-Cauley was told to stop any interaction with the label, but sources say he still worked for Knight, though on the sly (Sullivan, 2005). The revocation of McCauley's permit remains the only time LAPD has investigated an officer's involvement with the label, despite overwhelming evidence that many officers worked with the label, including the observations of a senior officer who responded to calls about armed gang members entering Death Row's CAN-AM studios in late June 1996. Among the "gang members" were off-duty officers, including McCauley.

Sources later described to detectives the standard way security was handled at Death Row: Knight had given his friend Reggie Wright $300,000 to start Wrightway Security, which would employ only black, off-duty officers, a move that not only let Death Row forgo the need to obtain gun permits, but that also placed cops on their payroll, almost guaranteeing that crimes would go uninvestigated and, in some cases, guaranteeing the best lookouts possible. Some officers, though, went far beyond basic security, as with officers David Mack, Rafael Perez, and Nino Durden.

DAVID MACK, RAFAEL PEREZ, AND THE RAMPART SCANDAL

But McCauley wasn't the only officer raising eyebrows among LAPD brass. Press reports reveal that detectives first noticed David Mack after he was arrested for what was then considered one of the biggest heists in Los Angeles history. Mack's girlfriend, Errolyn Romero, at the time was a Bank of America assistant manager, heading the branch just off the University of Southern California's campus. On November 6, 2007, while wearing a mask and brandishing a Tec-9 semiautomatic pistol he pulled from a shoulder holster beneath his suit jacket, Mack and two collaborators held up two tellers counting $722,000 in shrink-wrapped bundles, courtesy of the girlfriend, who had ordered $300,000 to be on hand that day. Mack reportedly screamed at the tellers not to touch the pagers or "I'll blow your heads off!" as they nervously counted the cash (Sullivan, 2005). The men left with the money, though the assistant manager who had ordered the extra banknotes was extensively questioned.

Within weeks, Romero confessed to police Mack's involvement, sliding his card across the interrogation table when asked, "Who is behind this?" He was arrested December 16, and the subsequent search of his house revealed more than $5,600 in small bills, $27,000 in receipts and deposit slips, and multiple guns, some registered, some unregistered. One of the guns used the same sort of slugs found in Wallace's body. They also found a shrine to the slain Shakur, complete with photos and candles. But what caught the investigators' attention most was a black Impala SS that perfectly matched the description of the car driven by Wallace's murderer. LAPD officers refused to examine the Impala. "The brass said no," Detective Russell Poole told reporter Randall Sullivan. "They didn't want to 'step on the FBI's toes.' What bullshit! The LAPD has never cared about stepping on the FBI's toes" (Sullivan, 2005).

According to sources, Mack told police to "take your best shot," as they read him his rights. Held at the Montebello City Jail, Mack reportedly told other inmates he was a member of the Mob Piru Bloods—the same gang to which Knight pledged allegiance—and claimed that more than $700,000 of the stolen cash had been spent in such a way that he would recoup nearly $1.5 million once released from jail. Knight and Mack grew up in the same part of Compton, and pictures proved Mack's connection to Death Row; he was at many of their events. Mack also used police radios similar to those used in Wallace's murder.

Almost as soon as Mack was imprisoned, Poole showed Damien "D-Roc" Butler a sheet of photos, asking if any of the faces were familiar. According to Sullivan, Butler immediately pointed to Mack, saying he was outside the door to the museum when the Bad Boy entourage first arrived at the party the night Wallace was killed. Even so, upper brass told homicide detectives to abandon that theory, as to not stir up any more controversy.

But police still closely monitored Mack's visitors, with the first being a man named Amir Muhammad, a friend of Mack from his college days, when both men were scholarship football players in the late 1970s at the University of Oregon. But his name was already familiar to police because a reliable jailhouse informant had earlier informed officers at the Los Angeles County Sheriff's Department that Wallace's murderer was a contract killer named Amir or Ashmir who was part of the Fruits of Islam security guard, men known for their neat appearances, closely cropped haircuts, and suits. The informant also told police that Knight had ordered the hit and that it was related to Shakur's murder. Muhammad's driver's license picture—copied at the time he visited Mack—was nearly identical to the composite drawing of Wallace's shooter, as described by witnesses. Detectives also learned that Muhammad was using a fake name; his legal name was Harry Billups, a moniker he had all but abandoned. He also used a false social security number and false address when he checked in at the prison.

But despite the mounting circumstantial evidence, Poole was told to leave the Mack angle alone and to look elsewhere, such as by investigating various gang connections or by reinterviewing witnesses.

As Poole conducted additional interviews with Shakur's former bodyguards, Kevin Hackie and Frank Alexander, he became more convinced of the link between Wallace's and Shakur's murders, a connection he felt certain was Knight. In one of the interviews, Alexander told Poole he felt that Knight had staged the attack on Orlando Anderson, a conviction based not only on his observations at the time but also on things said after Shakur's death. Alexander repeatedly told Poole he should interview Anderson, who had not talked to authorities since his defense of Knight's behavior on the stand months earlier. He also suggested Poole talk to Yafu Fula, a childhood friend of Shakur who was with the Death Row group on the deadly Las Vegas night. Fula told police at the time that he could finger the killer because he had caught a glimpse of the triggerman as he pulled away from Shakur's car (Sullivan, 2005).

Neither Anderson nor Fula was easy to find, and within months, both were killed. Anderson was found shot dead in his car in the parking lot of a Compton car wash in May 1998. Fula was shot to death in the hallway of a New Jersey public housing building just six months later.

"It just seemed incredibly convenient," Poole later told writer Randall Sullivan. "The best witness and main suspect in the murder of Tupac, both shot dead, while the case remained unsolved" (Sullivan, 2005).

That same year, Russell Poole was introduced to detective Rafael Perez, whose name appeared on a list of officers Mack had worked with over the years. The two had once worked together as undercover narcotics agents, and they were the two officers working a case that ended with the shooting death of a notorious drug dealer, Jesse Vincencio. Mack pulled the trigger and was later awarded LAPD's second highest honor, the Police Medal, for his work. At the ceremony, Perez claimed to owe his life to Mack, saying he would do anything for the officer. And, possibly, he did. It was Perez, as well as a third officer named Sammy Martin, who went with Mack to Las Vegas just after the bank robbery, the three staying in a $1,5000-a-night suite at the fancy Caesar's Palace, spending more than $20,000 on gambling, food, and liquor in a single weekend (*Frontline*, 2001).

As Poole continued to look into Perez, he began to connect the errant officer with several large drug deals, including one that involved stealing a massive amount of cocaine from the evidence room and later replacing it with Bisquick. The cocaine carried a street value of $800,000. He and his partner, Nino Durden, were moving large quantities of cocaine they found on the dealers they busted, and Perez was later believed to have sold drugs found on Vincencio's body, whose pager reportedly went off just as the officers stood over his dead body. The officers answered the page and finished the deal, some alleged.

LAPD officials soon gathered enough evidence against Perez to warrant an indictment, and in 1998 the case went to trial, and Perez faced a jury. But even with the stacks of evidence against the officer, the jury deadlocked, leaving the case in limbo, something that didn't work for the LAPD. "That hung jury changed the whole outlook of the investigation," Poole said. "Parks wanted this thing over by the end of the year, but when they lost that first trial, the chief panicked, thinking, 'We gotta do something fast.' So they started pushing to make a deal with Perez" (Sullivan, 2005, p. 227).

The consequences of the deal that was made still impact Los Angeles because Perez weaved a tale of corruption, greed, and murder that incriminated more than 70 officers who worked with LAPD's Rampart Division, a branch of the police department that largely served the areas west and northwest of downtown Los Angeles. The division also housed Los Angeles's CRASH division, or Community Resources against Street Hoodlums, an effort that targeted gang-related crime in the area, especially that of Hispanic gangs. Perez, now considered a hero for having exposed the corruption of the division, described in detail the hundreds of crimes he said happened, as well as a house where an elite group of unethical cops took their drugs, hookers, and cash, often entertaining rappers, including those from Death Row. Perez also claimed that gifts were given for murdering different gang members and that the upper brass always covered up the crimes. He always maintained, though, that Mack was not involved and that Mack was one of the last "good cops" remaining on the force (*Frontline*, 2001).

Los Angeles Police Chief Bernard Parks seem to buy Perez's story, despite there being almost no evidence to support his case and despite also his failing of five lie detector tests to confirm his statements. "We take Rafael Perez at this word," Parks told reporters and the Los Angeles City Council after placing at least 12 officers on suspension. Local papers, and especially the *Los Angeles Times*, cast the story as David versus Goliath, with Perez as the lone voice speaking against the massive malfeasance of the Rampart Division. As it was said and done, Perez was only to receive five years for cocaine theft, less any time served, and he received immunity for all the crimes he described.

Soon, though, more questions were raised. The house Perez described was never found, and in his testimonies about other officers, Perez seemed to change the details, conveniently "forgetting" a lot of what he'd already told authorities. In one particular case against officer Lawrence Martin, Perez offered a date of a crime that was implausible because one of the people involved was in prison at the time. Later, an attorney for Martin claimed Perez had "told so many lies that he's confused. He doesn't know what the truth is anymore" (Sullivan, 2005).

Even so, police officials still supported Perez's claims, though they now were only "seventy to eighty percent" sure of what he had said, as it had been confirmed by investigators. Even so, nearly all the officers suspended for their actions were later absolved because their crimes were not proved.

What *would* later be proved, though, was Perez and Durden's possible involvement with Wallace's murder, a connection that many believed involved David Mack. In September 1999, Mack was sentenced to 14 years for the bank heist, and police soon discarded theories that Mack was possibly involved in the murder, something Detective Poole would later tell reporters was a strong reason for his finally quitting the force, filing suit against the city for violation of his first amendment rights, when upper police management wouldn't let him tell what he'd learned. He knew there was some sort of cover-up because lengthy reports he prepared on the murder were often culled down to just a few pages, and he was often told to abandon leads. Poole felt that LAPD didn't want to pursue the individuals involved because the implications in the police station would reach farther than a few errant officers. Soon, higher-ups made statements on the investigation, leading many to think the inquiry into Wallace's murder was all but shelved.

In May 2000, *Los Angeles Times* reporter Chuck Philips wrote that the LAPD no longer believed Mack was possibly involved in Wallace's death, though Philips never explained why. Philips did quote authorities as saying that they wanted to interview Muhammad, whom they had yet to interview, but that they were unable to find him. But for the article, Philips interviewed Muhammad, easily tracking him down. What was missing from the article was how Muhammad was arrested for "firearm brandishing" in Chino, a nearby town, after pulling a gun on his ex-girlfriend and her boyfriend while in traffic. Police found an unregistered Beretta on Muhammad, who gave authorities a fake driver's license. But he was only ticketed for carrying a concealed weapon, a charge that was expunged from his record two years later. He was never questioned about Mack, or about Wallace's murder. Within a week of his arrest, his ex-girlfriend and her boyfriend were found dead, bullets lodged in their heads.

"I'm not a murderer, I'm a mortgage broker," Philips reported Muhammad as saying, in reference to Wallace's murder. Because of this interview, the *Los Angeles Times* became heavily embroiled in the controversy surrounding Wallace's death and Mack's possible involvement, having published many stories on the subject that took notable stances, with an earlier article claiming that Mack and Muhammad were suspected in Wallace's murder and a later one claiming the men were not involved, both causing a discernible split in the newsroom. This chasm was heavily discussed by other publications, including *Brill's Content* and Los Angeles–area alternative weeklies. All reporters involved—mainly Chuck Philips, Matt Lait, and Scott Glover—maintain that their articles are factually correct, even if they contradict each other. But many blame the LAPD for the discrepancy in information because the police department later gave similar statements to the *Washington Post*, only to later recant.

WITNESSES EMERGE

More sources continued to come forward claiming a man named Mack, sometimes called D-Mack (Mack's street name), was responsible for

Wallace's murder, or at least knew who was responsible. Another source turned in a piece of jailhouse correspondence that included Mack's signature, as well as the letters "MOB," or Members of Blood.

Some of the best witnesses to the shooting—Combs, Butler, and their bodyguards—gave only the most basic information and provided police with enough information to draw a composite picture of the assailant, but little more. After the Bad Boy group returned to New York, Combs would answer questions only through his attorney and reportedly told his staff that if they talked to police, they would be fired (Sullivan, 2005).

But despite Combs's warnings, one man did step forward: Combs's former bodyguard, Eugene Deal. A New York State parole officer, Deal exuded a sense of honesty in his answers to the many questions police officers had, often providing as much detail as possible. Through Deal's testimony, Poole largely discarded the still-prevalent theory that Wallace's death was a gang hit ordered by the Crips in retaliation for an unpaid bill, telling officers that there were no gang issues that night and that the members of the Crips who were at the Peterson Museum, most notably those with DJ Quik, showed Wallace respect. Deal did note, though, that a man who looked to be with the Nation of Islam security team was around and watched Combs and Wallace with an intense curiosity. When the group left the party, this man was standing just outside the door, falling into step behind them, Deal said. He then turned, walking toward the area from which the Impala—the murder car—would soon come. Though Deal never saw any photos to identify this person, Nick Broomfield, director of the 2002 documentary *Biggie & Tupac*, showed him several, including one of Amir Muhammad that was mixed in with the others. Deal immediately gestured to Amir's photo, saying, "That's him right there"

And as witnesses came forward, one more stuck out for investigators and attorneys, a man named Mario Ha'mmonds. Ha'mmonds was both a felon and an informant, having assisted the FBI on many cases since first working with them in the early 1990s. Just after Wallace was killed, Ha'mmonds' name was passed along to the LAPD because he and Suge Knight had been friends while in prison at California Men's Colony in San Luis Obispo.

Dying from liver cancer and in a wheelchair while recovering from a broken neck, Ha'mmonds had spent more than half his life in prison—26 of his 49 years—and was considered one of the tougher men in prison, having been a part of the notorious Black Guerrilla Family prison gang. Although he had once owned part of the small hip-hop label Lock Records, he had spent more time working as an enforcer for one of the deadliest drug lords in California, later becoming a member of a Nation of Islam splinter group called the Five Percenters, men who believed their religious convictions gave them justification for committing crimes. For whatever reason, whether the reward money or some desire to go legitimate, Ha'mmonds offered his help to the FBI, who happily accepted. He most often assisted on investigations surrounding Suge Knight and Death Row Records, having met Knight through Shakur, whom Ha'mmonds knew from living in Marin City. The two ran into each other again at a Holyfield–Bowe heavyweight title fight in November 1995, and Ha'mmonds spent the weekend with Knight, Shakur, Snoop, and several others, gambling in casinos and holding court in the backroom of Knight's Club 662. It was there Knight first mentioned Wallace.

According to later news articles, Knight met with Ha'mmonds alone, and after some small talk about Ha'mmonds' background and some common friends they had, they had the following conversation, as later recalled by Ha'mmonds:

> "He mentioned Christopher Wallace—Biggie Smalls—and he say, 'You know, that fat punk is giving me a lot of lip and a lot of shit on the East Coast. You think you can handle it?' By 'handle it,' meaning, can you arrange or do—assassinate—Christopher Wallace, Biggie Smalls? I told him no." Knight seemed very disappointed: "He say, 'Aww, I thought you was hard, man.'" (Sullivan, 2005)

Despite his refusal to take Wallace out, Ha'mmonds still spent the weekend with Knight and met several of his other friends, including a man named Amir Muhammad, who greeted Ha'mmonds in fluid Arabic, a sign of his connection to the Nation of Islam.

Once back in Los Angeles, the two met again at a video shoot, where Knight reportedly told him that officers from the LAPD protected them during busts, later introducing Ha'mmonds to Mack, whom Knight claimed to be part of his security. Later, Ha'mmonds and Knight lived just steps from each other, in the same cellblock at San Luis Obispo Men's Colony. Knight began to rely on Ha'mmonds for protection, claiming that the Rolling Sixties Crips wanted his head. Soon Ha'mmonds ran errands for him, and Knight, who was almost illiterate, relied on the man to tell him what correspondence. During this time, Knight claimed responsibility for Wallace's murder, bragging that his men took care of Wallace, but telling Ha'mmonds how his men weren't able to hit Combs with any of the bullets, reporter Randall Sullivan later wrote.

Although Knight never named who actually shot Wallace, he did mention several names in association with the murder, including those of David Mack, Amir Muhammad, and former Compton police officer Reggie Wright Jr., as well as rapper Big Sykes, a former member of Shakur's Outlawz. Over several weeks, more details emerged. As later reported by writer Randall Sullivan, Ha'mmonds told authorities that two women began hanging out with Combs and Wallace, giving regular updates on where the men were the night Wallace killed. Using cell phones, the group kept in constant contact, and when Wallace was vulnerable, the trigger was pulled. Knight also told Ha'mmonds that the murder wasn't related to Shakur's death but was instead all about money. Ha'mmonds later came to believe Knight was responsible for Shakur's murder as well, a theory that has become increasingly common as time goes on.

THE INVESTIGATION CONTINUES

With the increased press coverage of her son's murder, Voletta Wallace began to learn more about the investigation, having been relatively uninformed during the entire process. She always believed in Detective Russell Poole, but once he quit the force, she felt as if there was nobody at the LAPD who genuinely cared about solving her son's murder. Both *Rolling Stone* and *The New Yorker* ran lengthy stories on the murder and subsequent investigation, which many felt was largely hindered by the department's desire to keep controversies and cover-ups from being exposed.

Along with Faith Evans, Voletta Wallace soon hired Perry Sanders, a lawyer from Louisiana, to handle their case. Sanders was well known in his field as a fair, smart, clever man who stayed on a case until he felt justice was served. For Wallace, there seemed to be few other people who would be able to take on the LAPD. In June 2001, just after two rather lengthy exposes of the case were published, Sanders officially became involved. He took cases only on contingency, and he worried that this would be a costly affair that would take several years, but after reading the articles in *Rolling Stone* and *The New Yorker*, Sanders agreed. On April 9, 2002, they filed suit against the LAPD and former police chief Bernard Parks for "deliberate indifference" to Wallace's murder.

But as Sanders gathered facts about the murder and the police's possible involvement in it, he began to see many of the shortcomings that came from the investigation and a systematic series of cover-ups on behalf of upper management. Sanders felt sure they could prove a wrongful death suit, and Voletta Wallace soon agreed. She wanted to recoup some of the money she felt Christopher Wallace's children had lost when their father—a top rapper who had several years left in his career—was shot dead, possibly in a setup orchestrated by LAPD officers, most notably David Mack, Rafael Perez, and Nino Durden. Although the connection of Perez and Durden was still vague, both Sanders and Wallace felt sure they were involved.

WALLACE BLAMED FOR SHAKUR'S DEATH

But while Sanders and his team sifted through the mountain of evidence, the *Los Angeles Times* published a story that led to even greater controversy. On the six-year anniversary of Shakur's shooting, September 6, 2002, the paper published a front-page story with the bold headline "Who Shot Tupac Shakur?"

The article detailed at length the theory that Southside Crips, including Orlando Anderson, were responsible for Shakur's death. Anderson had already said time and again that he had had no involvement in Shakur's death, a stance he maintained until he himself was killed on May 28, 1998, in a drive-by at a Compton car wash. Having already been introduced in other publications, this theory was not new, though the details that reporter Chuck Philips provided were a bit different than any that had been offered before.

Philips claimed that it was Wallace who asked Anderson to be involved with the murder, personally handing over the gun that was to be used, a .40-caliber pistol, because he wanted Shakur killed with Wallace's own gun, with bullets he provided. The article states Wallace offered $1 million for the rapper's death, an amount to which the Crip readily agreed.

Philips also placed Wallace in Vegas the night of the murder, claiming he had a penthouse suite at the MGM Grand, one registered under a false name. There he allegedly held court with hired thugs and fellow East Coast rappers, all of whom agreed Shakur needed to die. Philips also asserted that it was the scuffle between Anderson and the Death Row crew that gave Wallace the idea that now was the time to take Shakur out.

Almost as soon as he knew Shakur was dead, Wallace returned to New York, Philips wrote, having only paid $50,000 of the $1 million he owed, which fit nicely with previous theories that Wallace was killed because of an unpaid debt, theories Philips himself had explored extensively in earlier articles.

But those close to Wallace insist he was not in Vegas that night, saying that he and Lil' Cease were watching the Tyson–Sheldon fight on pay-per-view at Wallace's home in Teaneck, New Jersey, only learning of Shakur's murder on the late night news. Cease—like many others—also pointed out that it would be nearly impossible for someone of Wallace's fame and size to slip in unnoticed, especially at an event that fellow rappers were attending. Media was on the lookout for these celebrities, and Wallace would have surely been spotted.

Critics of the article have always pointed out the lack of specific sources or information that led to Philips's assertions. He never names the gang members who supposedly confirmed Wallace's involvement, nor has any police officer gone on the record. Many also criticized the paper's timing, releasing the article on the anniversary of Tupak's shooting, claiming the plethora of graphics, maps, and timetables that complemented the sensational story were meant just to sell papers, not solve a crime. But Philips, a Pulitzer Prize–winning, well-respected reporter, has always defended his story, maintaining that the information published was true.

MISTRIAL

After three years of investigation, Voletta Wallace's day in court finally came in 2006. Testimony began in late June, and by the fourth day, Wallace and Sanders felt their case might be strong enough to win. They'd already shown what they felt was compelling evidence that the LAPD had systematically ignored facts and witness statements involving Wallace's murder investigation.

After a long day in court, Sanders checked his voice mail messages. One of the usual callers was his secretary back in Louisiana telling him three people had called claiming to have information on the murder. Sanders was used to these sort of calls; ever since he had taken on the case, people had come out of the woodwork with information they felt was relevant. One of the callers stood out, though: a man who did not leave his name. Sanders returned his call first.

After forcing Sanders to promise his involvement would remain absolutely anonymous, because he was a commanding officer at the LAPD, the man said that he was on the Board of Rights for the LAPD, the disciplinary committee that handled any inter-department issues. Though often closed to the public, these hearings are almost always held during business hours in a hearing room. This man, however, claimed to have been at a hearing held in the basement of the Parker Center, the LAPD headquarters, that evaluated the testimony of a prison inmate named Kenneth Boagni, testimony claiming that, while in jail, Raphael Perez had admitted to a number of crimes, including the murder of Christopher

Wallace. The caller gave specific names and dates that Sanders verified that night. The next morning, he arrived at court with a handwritten presentation on his new findings. The presiding judge—Florence-Marie Cooper—immediately adjourned court, pending further investigation.

Over the weekend, the LAPD's Robbery-Homicide division was on lockdown as Internal Affairs investigators sifted through desk drawers and file cabinets looking for any paperwork related to Boagni's testimony. Finally they found what they were looking for. Detective Steve Katz, who had taken over the investigation after Poole's departure, had stashed more than 200 pages of documents and testimony in two desk drawers. Among the papers was Boagni's sworn affidavit that Perez had told him about his work for Suge Knight and Death Row Records, much of which included overseeing large drug deals. The affidavit also indicates that Perez recounted his role in Wallace's murder, though that role still remains unclear.

By Monday, it was clear there was a cover-up, though the extent was still unknown. Cooper immediately called a mistrial, declaring that the LAPD and its investigators had deliberately concealed massive amounts of evidence for six years.

In April 2007, Voletta Wallace and Faith Evans filed another suit against the City of Los Angeles and LAPD officers Raphael Perez and Nino Durden, naming the two former partners as coconspirators in Wallace's murder. The suit claims that while on the job, Perez was a gang member working with Death Row Records. It also alleges that he "has made specific statements that he, together with David Mack, conspired to murder and participated in the murder of Christopher Wallace." This suit claims they have suffered an estimated $500 million in financial losses from Wallace's death.

Both officers were indicted during the Rampart scandal, and Mack, in jail for a bank robbery, was part of the original suit filed against the city Wallace's family, though they later took his name off the filings.

In a related suit, several LAPD detectives through the union Los Angeles Police Protective League filed suit against the city, asking that "warrantless searches" of their workplaces stop. The main defendants—chief William Bratton and former deputy chief Michael Berkow—had ordered other officers to rummage through the desks, waste baskets, and file folders of a few detectives associated with Wallace's murder investigation, looking for missing documents that Wallace family attorneys claimed should have been made available to all involved parties.

A sexual harassment lawsuit was also filed by LAPD officer Ya-May Christle, who claimed that many of her findings, as a part of the investigative team that reviewed Wallace-related files, were never sent to Sanders, as ordered by the court. She also alleged that promotions and assignments were given in exchange for sexual favors, fingering former LAPD deputy chief Michael Berkow as the main defendant. Berkow, now the chief of police in Savannah, Georgia, has never commented on either allegation.

In 2006, LAPD Chief William Bratton created a six-person taskforce to investigate Wallace's murder in an effort to repair some of the public's faith in the department after the case was so improperly handled before.

Chapter 9

THE LEGACY

As the controversy surrounding Wallace's death continues, so do the lives of those he affected. For Combs, Wallace's death brought increased attention to his own career. Following the massive success of the single "I'll Be Missing You," Combs's first album *No Way Out* debuted on the charts at no. 1, selling more than 500,000 copies the first week alone. The album's three singles—including "I'll Be Missing You"—placed high on the charts, keeping top positions for several weeks. And though he suffered great criticism for the excess he displayed in his songs and videos, the video for the single "Victory" remains today the most expensive to date.

After Wallace's death, Combs's life took a decidedly violent turn. In December 1997, he was arrested on charges of aggravated assault of Interscope executive Steve Stoute, who at the time managed Nas, whose video, "Hate Me Now," depicted Combs as being hung on a cross and crucified, a scene Combs had willingly filmed earlier that year. He claimed, though, that he later requested the image be removed and that Stoute's staunch refusal led to violence. Around that same time, gunfire stopped a recording session featuring Lil' Kim and Lil' Cease, though information on the shooting is scant (Harris, 2005).

Two years later, Combs was arrested on charges of weapons violations after he and then-girlfriend Jennifer Lopez left Manhattan nightclub Club New York amid gunfire. As cops descended on the scene, Combs reportedly asked his limo driver to hide his gun, offering him money. The driver immediately told police this, and bribery charges were added to his lengthening list of charges. Although Combs was later acquitted, Bad Boy artist Shyne, who was with Combs and Lopez at the time, was not, and he was sentenced to 10 years in prison. Tabloids named Shyne "Diddy's Fall Boy" because some newspapers reported that the rapper did nothing to defend his artist in court.

Controversy has always followed Combs, who changed his nickname from "Puffy" to "P. Diddy" to, finally, just "Diddy," after claiming the "P" got between him and his fans. (He is not allowed to use the name "Diddy" in the United Kingdom, though, since losing a rather expensive court case to another performer who has used the name for more than a decade.) After being convicted of assaulting Michigan television host Roger Mills, Combs announced he would release a gospel album, *Thank You,* though it never materialized. Soon after that, Combs was arrested on reckless driving charges in Miami and immediately began working on unusual, yet high-profile, collaborations, such as one song with icon David Bowie, which appeared on the soundtrack to the movie *Training Day.* Combs also worked with Britney Spears and N'Sync, opening for the latter on their Spring 2002 celebrity tour. Once back in New York, he signed to his Bad Boy label a girl pop group called Dreams. Later that year, he created an MTV reality show called *Making the Band 2,* a sequel of sorts to the network's first offering. Finalists on the show competed for a contract with Bad Boy. The show—and the musical group that formed during it—were repeatedly mocked by many people, most notably David Chappelle on his *Chappelle's Show,* which featured a now infamous skit ridiculing Combs and the performers. But Combs kept with it and in the third season created an all-girl pop group called Dannity Kane.

In 2004 Combs headed MTV's "Vote or Die" campaign drive, one meant to get younger voters to the polls. The campaign was highly criticized for the same reason Combs was often criticized—too much image with little substance; there were no discussions of actual issues or candidates, and instead just countless ads featuring performers like Combs as well as others, including starlet Paris Hilton, simply saying that people should vote. It was later revealed that neither Combs nor Hilton voted; neither one was registered. He has also been sued by a former tenant on claims he rented her a rat-infested apartment, as well as a talent agency on charges of unfair competition. Combs himself sued a writer he claimed was contractually bound to write his biography, and Combs settled out of court a $3 million lawsuit filed by his former limo driver, who claimed to have emotional distress over the incident involving his gun charges four years earlier (Strong, 2005). Terms of the lawsuit were not disclosed.

But the biggest controversy to follow Combs is what many consider an overcommercialization of hip-hop because Combs often samples heavily from pop songs, something that has been mocked in many ways, including

in *The Onion*, the satire newspaper that once ran an article with the headline "New Rap Song Samples 'Billie Jean' in Its Entirety, Adds Nothing,"
with a story that starts, "Noted rapper/producer Sean 'Puffy' Combs released his hotly anticipated new single Tuesday, 'Tha Kidd (Is Not My
Son),' which samples Michael Jackson's 1983 smash 'Billie Jean' in its
entirety and adds nothing." He has also been mocked for his guest appearances on many of the original songs, remixes, and videos of his artist,
having almost always appeared in the videos for Notorious B.I.G. songs,
as he has in almost every remix.

But even with the criticism, Combs remains on top and is considered
one of the world's most influential figures in both hip-hop and music as
a whole, and he is easily one of the wealthiest men in hip-hop, with an
estimated worth that ranges from $346 to $375 million, depending on the
source.

In recent years, Lil' Kim has found great wealth as well, having had
several top-selling albums as well as a Grammy award for her collaborative
remake of "Lady Marmalade," which held the no. 1 spot on the Billboard
Hot 100 for five weeks, making Kim the first female rapper in history to
achieve that feat. She has also modeled for several top designers, including Versace, and has received countless accolades for her work, including
her third album, *La Bella Mafia*, which received 4.5 of 5 "mics" in the
highly influential music magazine *The Source*.

But, as with most of the Bad Boy clan, her successes have not come
without trouble, and in March 2005, she was found guilty of conspiracy
and perjury after lying to a grand jury over a February 2001 shootout.
Kim and members of Junior M.A.F.I.A. were leaving New York's Hot 97,
WHQT-FM, after making an appearance as guest DJs at the all hip-hop
station. On their way out, they saw rival rappers Capone-N-Noreaga arriving. The two groups had been embroiled in a rivalry since Foxy Brown
made fun of Lil' Kim in the Capone-N-Noreaga track "Bang Bang" off their
2000 release *The Reunion*. Almost immediately, Damien "D-Roc" Butler
and friend Suif "Gutta" Jackson pulled their guns—two semiautomatic
weapons—and opened fire. Though no one was killed, almost two dozen
shots were fired, and one man was shot in his back.

In the resulting court case, Kim lied about being with Butler and Jackson, claiming to not even know Jackson well. But video surveillance tape
showed the three leaving the building together, and there were countless
pieces of evidence of Kim's friendship with Jackson. But both men admitted to having weapons and agreed to a plea bargain in exchange for testi-
fying against Kim, a move that led to the dissolution of Junior M.A.F.I.A.
At her sentencing, she cried while clutching a Bible, asking for leniency

for her wrongdoing. In July 2005, Kim was sentenced to one year and a day in the Philadelphia Detention Center. She had requested to go to a camp center in Connecticut to be closer to her mother, but instead was ordered to report to the Philadelphia Detention Center. In May 2006, Debbie Harry released a Lil' Kim tribute song called "Dirty and Deep" in protest of her conviction, though Kim was already in jail at the time.

As she packed for jail, her fourth album *The Naked Truth* was released, earning Kim the coveted 5 mic rating from *The Source*, the first such feat for a female rapper. This album also marked her fourth top 10 debut on the Billboard 200 charts, coming in at no. 6.

The lead-up to her imprisonment was well documented by BET and was televised in March 2006 on the show *Lil Kim: Countdown to Lockdown*. The show remains BET's highest-rated premiere, with 1.7 million viewers tuning in. Once released from prison, the cameras rolled again, and a show depicting her life after prison aired in 2007.

After Wallace's death, Faith Evans married manager Todd Russaw, later delivering her third child, Joshua. In 1998 she released the highly anticipated album *Keep the Faith*, which had two hit singles, "Love Like This" and "All Night Long," as well as the no. 1 R&B single "Never Gonna Let You Go." She released *Faithfully* and *The First Lady* in 2001 and 2005, respectively. *Faithfully* marked her exit from Bad Boy Records, with *The First Lady* being her first record at her new home label, Capitol Records.

Not long after her son's death, Voletta Wallace formed the Christopher Wallace Foundation, which offers books and other resources to Brooklyn children as a way to help them live productive lives that aren't gang-related. Its tagline is "Think B.I.G.," the same phrase used on the bumper stickers that promoted Wallace's album *Life after Death* before he died. The foundation is active in the community and has reportedly helped thousands of children. Voletta Wallace also actively participates in helping find her son's killer and often speaks out on the issue.

On the 10-year anniversary of Wallace's death, Suge Knight, then 42, told a *New York Post* reporter he now intended to permanently close Death Row, nearly 16 years after its inception. He said his decision was spurred by two sermons he heard at Compton's City of Refuge Church, where preachers Noel James and T. D. Jakes both relayed a message of leaving behind the past to instead embrace a more positive future.

Knight, who was released from prison in 2004, has battled financial troubles associated with Death Row for years, having lost a $107 million dollar case to Lydia Harris, who claimed her husband, Michael Harris, an imprisoned crack dealer, had cofounded the label and held a 50 percent stake in its profits. Knight had given Lydia Harris $1 million earlier, but she claimed that in no way repaid the debt Death Row owed her husband.

Knight sought bankruptcy protection in April 2006, claiming his debts far outweighed his assets. After the case began, one of his lawyers quit after receiving repeated death threats, as did the judge presiding over the case. The court has requested that Knight continue operating Death Row under the Chapter 11 reorganization, though Knight has asked for permission to sell his publishing rights, pay off creditors, and end the Death Row legacy.

"I want to take care of the creditors. I'm saying I don't want to keep living in the past, with the negativity," Knight told the *New York Post* reporter. "We shouldn't be constantly feeding negative energy to these kids. You can get rich with the devil's money, but you can only be happy with God's money."

LIFE AFTER DEATH

Once described as the "Savior of East Coast hip-hop," Christopher Wallace is considered one of the greatest artists of all time. Undoubtedly, his contributions to music span far beyond just a couple of well-received albums and instead stand as a testament to the power of a person's will to create from nothing something, in this case something that forever shaped the music that followed his. From the dark undertones of *Ready to Die* came one of hip-hop's brightest stars, a man who is still considered one of the most influential rappers in the genre's history.

Many credit Wallace with having the ability to be everything to every-body, a versatility evidenced in both *Ready to Die* and *Life after Death*. In one song he professes his stress over his mother's "cancer in the breast," and in another track, he holds a woman at gunpoint, demanding her "baby rings and the no. 1 mom pendant." In some lyrics, he boasts of his achievements hustling; in others, he condemns them, suicidal because he feels he isn't worth anything, and he is sure his mom wishes she would've had an abortion. But that was the thing about Wallace. He was charming while at the same time condescending, and self-deprecating even as he boasted. He was realistic the same as he was unattainable, this overweight man with a lazy eye whom somehow all the women found irresistible.

Wallace was also proclaimed King of New York, as he wrestled back hip-hop's spotlight from the West Coast's gangsta rap stranglehold to the East Coast's new style, that of mafia fantasies, told by Wallace in his trademark narrative way. After the release of Notorious B.I.G.'s first mainstream single, "Juicy," in 1994, his debut album *Ready to Die* was critically acclaimed internationally, and he even kick-started the career of Lil' Kim when he created his crew Junior M.A.F.I.A.

His life was steeped in controversy, but that is what made Wallace who he was: a clever, complex man whose short life—and brief four-year career—is arguably one of the brightest spots in music history, one that forever changed the landscape of rap.

BIBLIOGRAPHY

Associated Press. "LAPD Launching New Notorious BIG Task Force." August 3, 2006, http://www.msnbc.msn.com/id/14118674/.

Broomfield, Nick. *Biggie & Tupac*. United Kingdom: Optimum Home Entertainment (DVD), 2002.

Brown, Jake. *Ready to Die: The Story of Biggie Smalls, Notorious B.I.G., King of the World & New York City: Fast Money, Puff Daddy, Faith and Life after Death: The Unauthorized Biography*. Phoenix, AZ: Colossus Books, 2004.

Coker, Cheo Hodari. *Unbelievable: The Life, Death, and Afterlife of the Notorious B.I.G*. New York: Three Rivers Press, Random House, 2003.

Duncan, Andrea, Chairman Mao, Adam Matthews, Peter Relic, Leah Rose, and Vanessa Satten. "The Making of *Ready to Die*." *XXL*, March 2006.

Duvoisin, Marc, and Randall Sullivan. "L.A. Times Responds to Biggie Story." *Rolling Stone*, January 12, 2006.

Egere-Cooper, Matilda. "Notorious B.I.G.: An Album Too Far?" *The (London) Independent*, January 27, 2006.

Fisher, Ian. "On Rap Star's Final Ride, Homage Is Marred by a Scuffle." *New York Times*, March 19, 1997.

Frontline. "L.A.P.D. Blues." PBS. May 2001.

Gilmore, Mikal. "Puff Daddy Cometh." *Rolling Stone*, August 7, 1997. Golub, Jan. "Who Killed Biggie Smalls?" *Salon*, October 16, 2000, http://archive.salon.com/news/feature/2000/10/16/biggie/index.html.

———. "B.I.G. Trouble at the *Los Angeles Times*." *Salon*, October 16, 2000, http://archive.salon.com/news/features/2000/10/16/times/index.html.

Harris, Chris. "Lil' Kim Gets a Year and a Day in Prison."*MTV.com*, July 6, 2005, http://www.mtv.com/news/articles/1505262/20050706/lil_kim.jhtml.

Hirschberg, Lynn. "Does a Sugar Bear Bite?" *New York Times Magazine*, January 14, 1996.

James, George. "Rapper Faces Prison Term for Sex Abuse." *New York Times*, February 8, 1995.

Jones, Charisse. "Still Hanging in the Hood." *New York Times*, September 24, 1995.

Lait, Matt, and Scott Glover. "Ex-LAPD Officer Is Suspect in Rapper's Slaying, Records Show." *Los Angeles Times*, December 9, 1999.

Mukherjee, Tiarra. "Un-derstanding Lance Rivera." *Rolling Stone*, August 6, 1998.

"Paper Investigates Rapper Murder." *BBC News Online*, September 6, 2002, http://news.bbc.co.uk/2/hi/entertainment/1287596.stm.

Philips, Chuck. "Gangsta Rap Performer Notorious B.I.G. Slain." *Los Angeles Times*, March 10, 1997.

———. "LAPD Renews Search for Rapper's Killer." *Los Angeles Times*, July 31, 2006.

———. "Slain Rapper's Family Keeps Pushing Suit." *Los Angeles Times*, February 7, 2007.

Powell, Kevin. "Ready to Live." *Vibe*, April 1995.

———. "Live from Death Row." *Vibe*, February 1996.

"Rap's Stormy Knight." *BBC News Online*, April 23, 2001, http://news.bbc.co.uk/2/hi/entertainment/1287596.stm.

Reid, Shaheem. "Notorious B.I.G.: In His Own Words, and Those of His Friends." *MTV News*, March 7, 2007.

———. "Notorious B.I.G. Wrongful-Death Case Declared a Mistrial." *MTV News Online*, July 5, 2005, http://www.mtv.com/news/articles/1505321/20050706/notorious_big.jhtml.

"Review: *Ready to Die*." *Q* Magazine, December 1994.

Ro, Ronin. *Bad Boy: The Influence of Sean "Puffy" Combs on the Music Industry*. New York: Atria, 2001.

———. *Have Gun Will Travel: The Spectacular Rise and Violent Fall of Death Row Records*. Hattiesburg, MS: Main Street Books, 1999.

Scott, Cathy. *The Murder of Biggie Smalls*. London: Plexus Publishing Ltd, 2001.

"Stakes Is High." *Vibe*, September 1996.

Strong, Nolan. "Diddy and Random House Settle; Random House not Publishing Memoirs." *All Hip Hop*, July 13, 2005, http://allhiphop.com/blogs/news/archive/2005/07/13/18130163.aspx.

Sullivan, Randall. *LAbyrinth: A Detective Investigates the Murders of Tupac Shakur and Notorious B.I.G., the Implication of Death Row Records' Suge Knight, and the Origins of the Los Angeles Police Scandal*. New York: Grove Press, 2003.

————. "The Unsolved Mystery of the Notorious B.I.G." *Rolling Stone*, December 5, 2005.

Touré. "Biggie Smalls; Rap's Man of the Moment." *New York Times*, December 18, 1994.

U.S. Department of Justice. "CIA-Contra-Crack Cocaine Controversy: A Review of the Justice Department's Investigations and Prosecutions." Washington, D.C.: December 1997.

Wallace, Voletta, and Tremell McKenzie. *Biggie: Voletta Wallace Remembers Her Son, Christopher Wallace, aka Notorious B.I.G.* New York: Atria, 2005.

Weiner, Jonah. "33 Things You Should Know about Tupac Shakur." *Blender*, January/February 2004.

INDEX